Whitehall Paper 97

War by Others' Means
Delivering Effective Partner Force Capacity Building

A new era of great power competition places a strategic premium on the efficiency with which states can pursue their aims. There is therefore likely to be an expanded scope for partnered operations. Partner force capacity building has a long history, with very mixed results, yet there is little historical memory in the institutions tasked with carrying it out. *War by Others' Means* uses archival research, interviews with practitioners, and observation of capacity building to understand why states undertake it, how they should select, train and equip their partners, and how they should manage the generation and withdrawal of trainers.

War by Others' Means
Delivering Effective Partner Force Capacity Building

By: Jack Watling and Nick Reynolds

Published 2020

ISBN: 9780367766405

Mapping the Issues

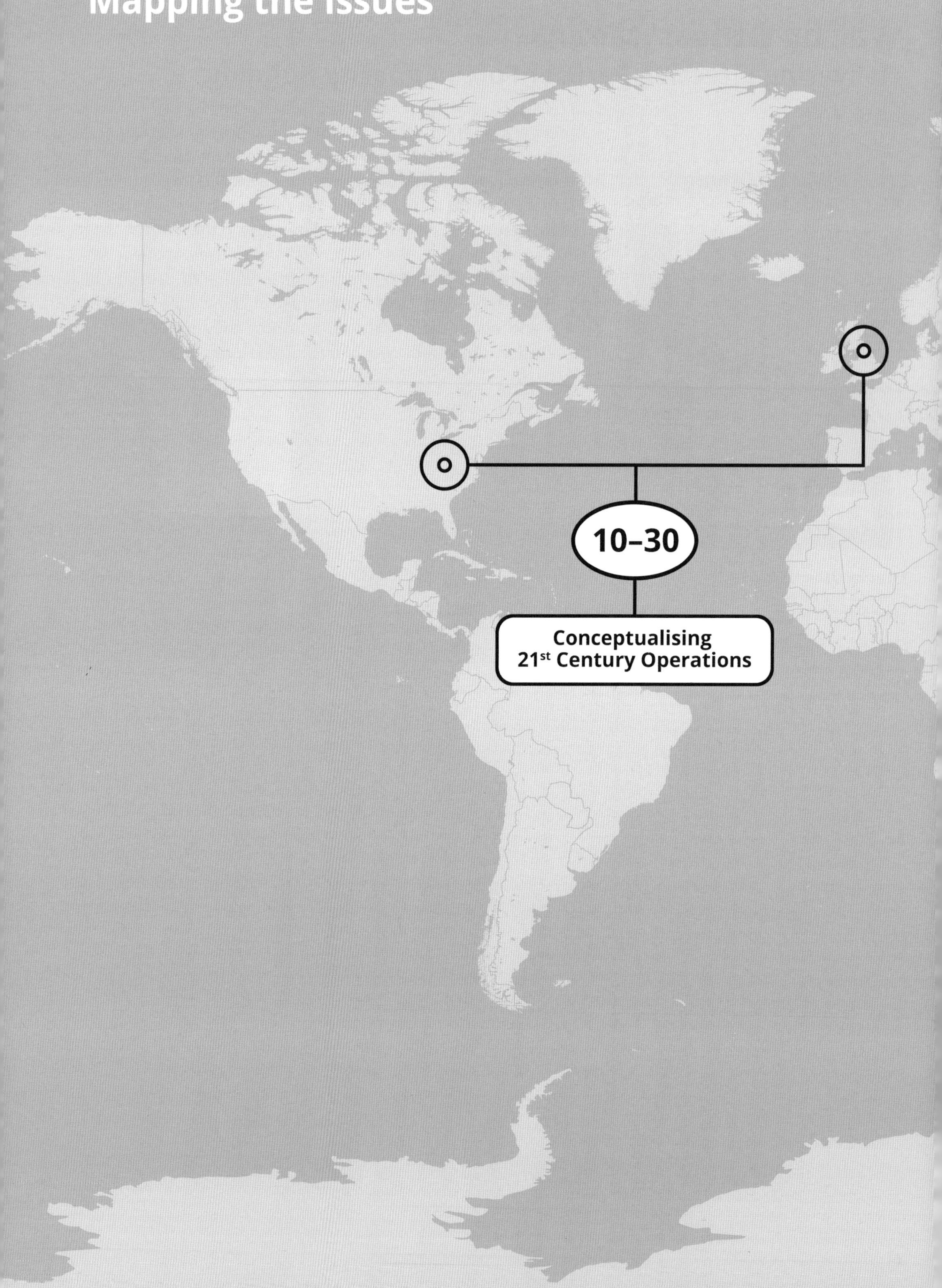

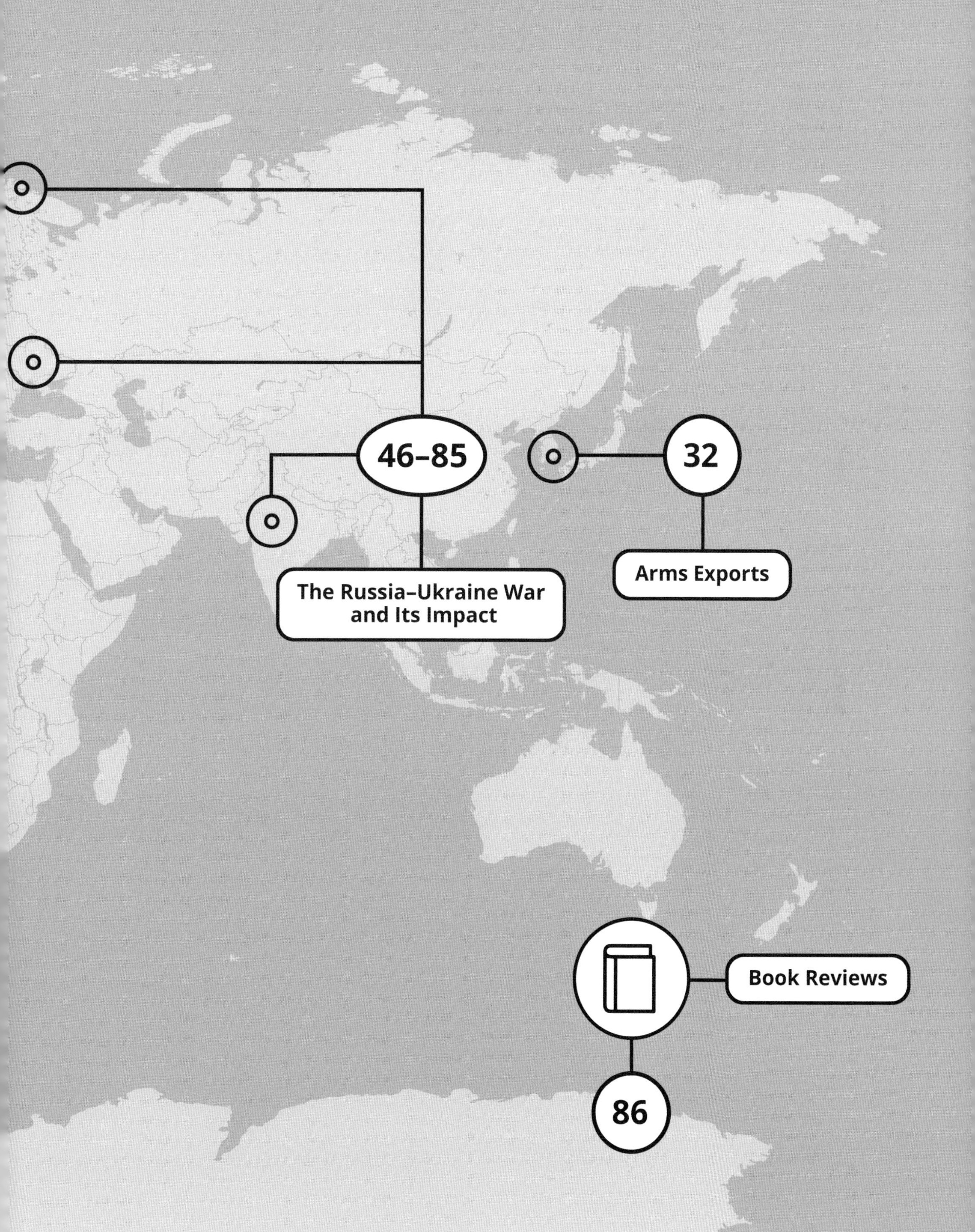
46–85
32
The Russia–Ukraine War and Its Impact
Arms Exports
Book Reviews
86

Contents

RUSI Journal

Cover image: US Naval Special Warfare Operators (SEALS) and Explosive Ordnance Disposal Mobile Unit 12 sailors rappel from an MH-60S Nighthawk helicopter.
Courtesy of APFootage / Alamy Stock Photo

The RUSI Journal
Independent thinking on defence and security

Published seven times per year

First published 1857
www.rusi.org

The *RUSI Journal* is a world-leading journal on defence and security. First published in 1857, it is the oldest publication of its kind, bringing scholars, decision-makers and practitioners together in a unique forum that combines academic rigour with policy relevance.

The publication embodies a global perspective on issues relevant to peace and security. The *Journal*'s fundamental mission is to present high-quality, policy-relevant research in an accessible manner.

Aims and Scope

The *RUSI Journal* challenges orthodox assumptions and brings fresh perspectives to the major security questions of the day. The peer-reviewed Research Articles bring original, high-quality analysis to current debates. The *Journal* also offers other formats, such as Comments and Features, which provide highly accessible and informed analysis of global peace and security issues to policymakers, scholars, students, practitioners and the wider public.

A broad range of topics feature within the *Journal*, including: war, strategy and military history; contemporary geopolitics; the security situation in unstable or at-risk parts of the world; global and local security trends; climate and environmental security; terrorism and counterterrorism; the legal and ethical questions of armed action; defence and national decision-making; the relationships between the doctrine and activities of the military and other deployable instruments of national power; the economic and industrial underpinnings of defence; the policy implications of military technology; and domestic security and resilience.

Peer Review Statement

All content is reviewed by the Editor and Book Reviews Editor. The *Journal*'s editorial team may also seek feedback from subject-matter experts for certain content types, including Comments and Features. In addition, all Research Articles and Review Essays published in the *RUSI Journal* are subject to an anonymous double-blind review process by external referees and members of the *Journal*'s Editorial Board. Publication in the *Journal* is at the discretion of the Editor.

Editorial Policy

Authors alone are responsible for the content of their respective contributions. It is the policy of the *Journal* to give the fullest freedom to contributors and correspondents to express their opinions. Only by doing so can the Institute carry out the terms of its charter. The opinions and conclusions written by RUSI staff and fellows do not necessarily represent the views of the Royal United Services Institute.

Royal United Services Institute for Defence and Security Studies
Whitehall
London SW1A 2ET
United Kingdom

+44 (0)20 7747 2600
www.rusi.org
publications@rusi.org

RUSI is a registered charity (No. 210639)

The RUSI Journal is published on behalf of RUSI by Routledge Journals, an imprint of
Taylor and Francis
4 Park Square
Milton Park
Abingdon
Oxfordshire OX14 4RN
United Kingdom

ISSN 0307-1847

Printed and bound by Henry Ling Ltd., UK

Subscriptions

All individual and corporate members of RUSI receive a subscription to the Journal.
Non-members can subscribe via Taylor & Francis: www.tandfonline.com
USA/Canada: Taylor & Francis Inc.
Journals Department, 530 Walnut Street, Suite 850, Philadelphia, PA 19106, USA
UK/Rest of World: Routledge Journals
T&F Customer Services, T&F Informa UK Ltd, Sheepen Place, Colchester, Essex, CO3 3LP, UK

Submissions

The Editor welcomes unsolicited manuscripts on issues of British and international defence and security.

Full guidelines can be found on the back page of each print edition, and also on the RUSI website at www.rusi.org/explore-our-research/publications/rusi-journal/contributor-guidelines

Editor's Note

The war in Ukraine, now in its second year, has fuelled an already intense debate on what type of confrontations we should expect and prepare for in the coming years. Even before Russia's full-scale invasion, the discussion had shifted to understanding the realities of great power rivalry and strategic competition, and away from the emphasis on counterinsurgency, expeditionary warfare and counterterrorism that consumed much of the early years of this century. Russia and China are seeking to redraw the established parameters of the global order, and while Russia's invasion of Ukraine shows a decided willingness to start violent military confrontation of a 20th-century ilk, new technologies and domains overlay and expand the types and levels of engagement at which states must be able to compete.

In this complex arena, what type of resources, doctrine and concepts are most suited to the mid-21st century, and how can Western states best prepare not only for the wars of today, but the wars of tomorrow? Two articles in this issue explore how to think through such questions in specific contexts. David H Ucko looks at the changing role of special operations forces and discusses the opportunities and limitations of them, focusing on how they can best be harnessed within US strategic culture. In an essay reflecting on the role of the Royal Marines from a close-combat viewpoint, James White explores some of the challenges of developing sound tactical concepts for the effective organisation and deployment of this elite force.

These rapid changes are also affecting the weapons systems being developed and sold around the world, alongside commercial, dual-use technologies. As new actors emerge on the market, Shirzad Azad analyses South Korea's ascendance as an important actor in the Middle Eastern arms market over the past three decades.

Among the many dimensions of the war in Ukraine, the media has often focused on the role of foreign volunteers that have travelled to Ukraine to join its efforts against the invasion – scrutinising their motivations and inquiring into their political allegiances and networks. Matteo Pugliese's article presents some preliminary findings on the International Legion's recruits. Based on conversations with members of the Legion, he paints a diverse and complex picture of the many foreign volunteers that have joined Ukraine's fight, and their reasons for doing so.

The war does of course reverberate across the world in very different ways, and the reaction to Russia's invasion outside Western allies has been far from unanimous. India in particular has been treading a fine line in its relations with both Russia and the West. Shubhrajeet Konwer analyses India's position during the first year of the war, looking at its approach to maintaining its relations with Russia and the US, with an eye to China and the war's impact on the regional balance of power.

Finally, Runar Spansvoll considers the array of tools that Russia has used, and continues to employ, to further its foreign and security policy outside of direct military action, focusing on Russian sub-threshold activities in neighbouring Norway. ■

Dr Emma De Angelis
Editor

Image: Generative AI image of silhouetted soldiers.
Courtesy of Let's-Get-Creative / Adobe Stock

DOI: 10.1080/03071847.2023.2229201

The Role and Limits of Special Operations in Strategic Competition
The Right Force for the Right Mission

David H Ucko

As the US shifts from counterterrorism to strategic competition against state rivals, the role of its special operations forces is also changing. David H Ucko explores the promise and limitations of special operations in this new era, identifying their contribution but also the need for a broader response. Indeed, because strategic competition is primarily non-violent, with instruments of state weaponised to offset military inferiority, an effective response will similarly require a diversification of statecraft away from the military. This requirement poses challenges to an American strategic culture still reliant on armed superiority and, for two decades, direct action by elite forces.

The US special operations community finds itself in a delicate transition. Following two decades of engagement, predominantly in counterterrorism and counterinsurgency, it is now recasting itself as relevant to a new strategic era, one in which the US's chief adversaries are state governments rather than armed groups. The transition is delicate primarily because of uncertainty as to what special operations forces (SOF) is for – or what makes it special. On the one hand, there is the risk of underuse, based on policymakers' poor grasp of SOF's various competences and potential. On the other, perceived ignorance as to SOF's quality has led the special operations community to promote what their forces can do, leading to a risk of overuse, as these elite forces sign up for or are handed an ever-growing list of unfamiliar and potentially high-risk engagements. Finding a balance between these two poles is necessary but made more difficult by the deliberate ambiguity of the great power competition in which the US finds itself.

This backdrop warrants an honest exchange on SOF's role in great power competition, so that its value is not squandered, either through a dearth or excess of imagination. This article makes four key arguments. First, it posits that SOF consolidates its core strengths, particularly in irregular warfare, which is highly relevant to the strategic competition underway. Specific attention is paid to SOF's efforts to boost the resilience and resistance potential of frontline states, work that builds on SOF's experience with and responsibility for countering and sponsoring insurgency. In a similar vein, its international partnerships and persistent engagement will also be key.

Second, beyond this broad range of complex and demanding tasks, there are limits to what one should expect from SOF in great power competition. The reasons for restraint are based on inevitable limits on SOF's bandwidth, the trade-offs inherent to adding more to an already full plate, and the nature of the competition, which in most respects remains a non-military phenomenon. This does not mean that SOF cannot play valuable supporting roles, but these should specifically increase the reach and access of non-military instruments of power, which have the authority and knowhow, and should be resourced for the associated tasks.

Third, the exigences of interagency integration should also drive engagement in irregular warfare. There is a tendency within the US government to delegate irregular warfare to the special operations community – because general-purpose forces privilege conventional combat capabilities and the

A 10th Special Forces Group soldier participates in a live fire training exercise at the Panzer Range Complex, Germany, January 2021. *Courtesy of US Army / Jason Johnston*

rest of the government is seldom included in the related discourse or planning.[1] And yet, irregular warfare is fundamentally about legitimacy, politics and blended lines of effort and so cannot be left to what is, after all, a military force – no matter how special. Senior leaders within the special operations community recognise this point, and promising initiatives such as the Irregular Warfare Center seek to address it, but institutionalising a national, coordinated approach to irregular warfare remains a far-off target.[2] Meanwhile, the required shift in mindset is made only more urgent given SOF's growing focus on resilience and resistance against foreign subversion, because the lines of effort against which such efforts seek to protect will, in many cases, be non-military instead of (or as well as) military. In other words, even within irregular warfare, SOF relies upon and can scarcely be strategically significant without the presence of others.[3]

Finally, though achieving an aware, integrated and capable joint and interagency force would be no small feat, a final question concerns the strategic direction necessary to meet the ends of policy. It is difficult to say what body within the US government currently sets this strategy, what the US is competing for, and how it defines success. The opacity leads

1. On the delegation of irregular warfare to the special operations community, see David H Ucko, *The New Counterinsurgency Era: Transforming the U.S. Military for Modern Wars* (Washington, DC: Georgetown University Press, 2009), pp. 36–55, 89–94. On the exclusion of the interagency from these conversations, see Lew Irwin, 'Filling Irregular Warfare's Interagency Gaps', *The US Army War College Quarterly: Parameters* (Vol. 39, No. 3, 1 August 2009); Charles T Cleveland and Daniel Egel, *The American Way of Irregular War: An Analytical Memoir*, PE-A301-1 (Santa Monica, CA: RAND Corporation, 2020), pp. 210–12.
2. On senior-level advocacy, see (most recently), Bryan P Fenton, 'How Special Operations Forces Must Meet the Challenges of a New Era', *Defense One*, 11 May 2023. On the Irregular Warfare Center, see Kevin D Stringer and Madison Urban, 'Irregular Warfare Campaigning and the Irregular Warfare Center', *Irregular Warfare Center: Insights* (Vol. 1, No. 1, 1 December 2022).
3. Though the ultimate 'SOF Truth' (the principles of the special operations community) correctly notes that 'most special operations require non-SOF support', it is arguably more important that SOF support a national strategy and approach. USSOCOM, 'SOF Truths', <https://www.socom.mil/about/sof-truths>, accessed 25 May 2023.

DOI: 10.1080/03071847.2023.2219701

to a lack of focus and prioritisation, both within and across government. Beyond any proper delineation of missions and tasks, the most fundamental need is therefore for greater clarity as to the US's purpose and reasons for competing.

Strategic Context

Since 2017, the US has shifted its priorities away from counterterrorism and towards great power competition, now often referred to as 'strategic competition'. The shift came in response to the greater assertiveness and incremental success of the People's Republic of China and the Russian Federation in challenging the international norms and order promoted by the US. How to respond is now the focus of the US national security enterprise, but it is a question compounded by the varied and global method of attack.

> China and Russia have sought to soften up, subvert, and ultimately flip the international system in their favour

Indeed, in contrast with the war raging in Ukraine, great power competition is for the most part a non-violent struggle, wherein the US's rivals deliberately seek to avoid its military strengths. Instead, the strategy used by these actors targets societal, information and economic areas where US capacity to deter and respond is less advanced. Though anchored in a shared awareness of underlying military realities, the theory of success relies on incremental gains, under the threshold of armed conflict, until new facts have been created and become difficult to reverse.

As part of this indirect attack, China and Russia have sought to soften up, subvert, and ultimately flip the international system in their favour. Individual countries are targeted, with carrots as well as sticks, to build informal blocks of pro-Chinese or pro-Russian support. In tandem, US influence wanes, along with its legitimacy and power. Methods range from the relatively peaceful, such as infrastructural development and charm offensives, to more coercive ones, such as 'debt-trap' diplomacy, cyber attacks, or the use of disinformation and political infiltration. Only in a few instances has the strategy relied on military aggression, such as that seen in Ukraine. Further armed confrontation is of course possible, but would-be adversaries will have learned from Vladimir Putin's mistake not to attack until the correct conditions have been set by other means.

SOF Core Activities in Great Power Competition

As the US observes China and Russia subverting its international leadership, what is SOF's role in turning the tide? The good news is that its core activities are also relevant in this new strategic environment. Beyond its well-publicised strikes and covert activities in denied areas, which can be invaluable in several different ways, the bulk of SOF's contribution resides in its specialisation in irregular warfare. Though traditionally concerned with non-state threats and focused on counterinsurgency and counterterrorism, irregular warfare also captures the playbook used by Russia, China and others competing with the US. Doctrine explains how irregular warfare 'favors indirect and asymmetric approaches' to direct military confrontation and seeks 'to erode an adversary's power, influence, and will'. Furthermore, irregular warfare is fundamentally 'a struggle [...] to influence populations and affect legitimacy', which speaks to the strategic competition at hand: an international struggle for the right to lead and to shape new and long-lasting political realities.[4]

Given this overlap, SOF's irregular warfare expertise can also be relevant in an era of strategic competition – though some tweaks are needed.[5] In recent years, SOF has broadened its thinking on foreign internal defence (FID) and unconventional warfare – two irregular warfare missions and SOF core activities. Whereas FID traditionally meant aiding a friendly government against an insurgency, SOF now looks upon it to boost a country's 'resilience' against foreign-sponsored proxies, modes of disinformation or political infiltration.

4. US Department of Defense, 'Summary of the Irregular Warfare Annex to the National Defense Strategy', 2 October 2020, p. 2. For the overlap, and distinctions, between state and non-state irregular warfare challenges, see David H Ucko and Thomas A Marks, *Crafting Strategy for Irregular Warfare: A Framework for Analysis and Action*, 2nd edition (Washington, DC: National Defense University Press, 2022), pp. 8–15.

5. For discussion, see Kevin Bilms, 'What's in a Name? Reimagining Irregular Warfare Activities for Competition', *War on the Rocks*, 15 January 2021; Stephen Watts et al., *Countering Russia: The Role of Special Operations Forces in Strategic Competition*, Rand Research Report, RR-A412-1 (Santa Monica, CA: RAND Corporation, 2021).

Through various Security Force Assistance and FID programmes, the US special operations community is actively engaged in boosting their counterparts in Eastern Europe to ensure greater resilience against a wide range of Russian provocations. The central idea is that a more resilient nation is a greater defence and deterrent against irregular attack and, also, a promising foundation for resistance should the country's sovereignty become threatened.[6]

On the latter, whereas unconventional warfare traditionally implied sponsoring an insurgency against an illicit or occupying government, SOF now looks upon this work as supporting 'resistance' capabilities within states facing foreign invasion. The current assistance to Ukraine against the Russian invasion illustrates the approach and its importance, though it bears noting that SOF was active in Ukraine several years before the February 2022 escalation.[7] This method finds precedent in the US sponsorship of Afghan mujahideen in countering the Soviet Union, and in various resistance efforts during the Second World War. The rediscovery of this type of work has led Special Operations Command Europe (SOCEUR), working with various European academic and military partners, to produce, in 2020, the Resistance Operating Concept (ROC), which now acts as a theoretical guidebook for these efforts.[8]

Building resilience and resistance hands SOF a major role in strategic competition, given Russian and Chinese subversion of vulnerable states and threats to neighbouring countries. However, these are demanding tasks, requiring institutional readiness and protracted partnerships. After 20 years of counterterrorism, where SOF engaged heavily in direct action, there is a need to rebalance in favour of FID and unconventional warfare, and to develop the skills they call for within a new strategic environment.[9] These include language skills, cultural know-how, political awareness and strategic acumen – all at scale – with major implications for SOF recruitment and career tracks. The decline of high-tempo counterterrorism provides an opportunity, but the challenge of reform is significant. As former United States Special Operations Command (USSOCOM) commander Eric T Olson argues, it remains 'extremely difficult [...] to create a SOF operator who knows the people, languages, terrain, climate, politics, and religions of a micro-region without hurting his/her chances for promotion to the top ranks'.[10]

Beyond FID and unconventional warfare, SOF's work with irregular warfare brings other relevant capabilities. Because irregular warfare 'favors indirect approaches' (that is, working through partners and proxies), SOF has a strong tradition of engagement at the state level and below. Its involvement in security force assistance is key, as it creates bonds with all those receiving such support. It also means that SOF is in over 80 countries on any given day, providing the US an opportunity to sense and shape the environment. Developing and extending these networks will help mobilise common fronts against common threats and, as irregular warfare is ultimately a struggle for legitimacy, such work is key.[11]

---

6. Craig A Thompson, 'SOF Utilization in Contemporary Competitive Spaces', *Special Operations Journal* (Vol. 6, No. 2, July 2020), p. 102; Otto C Fiala, *ROC: Resistance Operating Concept* (MacDill AFB, FL: JSOU Press, 2020), pp. 7–18.
7. See Stavros Atlamazoglou, 'Ukrainian Special-Operations Forces Doubled in Size While Training with the US, Top US Special-Ops Commander Says', *Business Insider*, 9 June 2022. Similar initiatives in Taiwan occasionally make it to the news, though US officials typically deny these reports. See Joseph Trevithick, 'American Forces Have been Quietly Deployed to Taiwan with Increasing Regularity: Report', *The Drive*, 7 October 2021, <https://www.thedrive.com/the-war-zone/42658/american-forces-have-been-quietly-deployed-to-taiwan-with-increasing-regularity-report>, accessed 22 May 2023.
8. For discussion, see Derek Jones and J Bryant Love, 'Resilience and Resistance 2.0: Initial Lessons of Ukraine and the Implications of Resilience and Resistance Efforts to Deter and Respond to Invasion and Occupation by Revisionist Powers', *Bezpieczeństwo. Teoria i Praktyka* (No. 3, August 2022), pp. 21–40. For the resistance operating concept, see Fiala, *ROC: Resistance Operating Concept*.
9. United States Special Operations Command, 'Comprehensive Review', 23 January 2020, p. 39, <https://sof.news/pubs/USSOCOM-Comprehensive-Ethics-Review-Report-January-2020.pdf>, accessed 19 May 2023.
10. Admiral Olson therefore recommends that the USSOCOM commander be granted 'the authority to manage selected personnel to very high levels of focused expertise without damaging their careers', perhaps via 'the development of alternative career paths'. See Eric T Olson, 'USSOCOM and SOF: War Around the Edges', *Journal of National Security Law and Policy* (Vol. 12, No. 71, October 2021), p. 78.
11. As General Richard D Clarke, Commander of SOCOM, explains, 'USSOCOM maintains a global network of liaison officers and exchange officers with Allied and international SOF. At our headquarters alone, we host exchange officers and foreign liaison officers from 28 Allied and partnered nations, offering an unrivaled ability to provide options to understand and act worldwide'. See Special Operations Command, 'Statement of General Richard D. Clarke, USA, Commander, United States Special Operations Command', Washington DC, 5 April 2022, p. 5, <https://www.congress.gov/117/meeting/house/114577/witnesses/HHRG-117-AP02-Wstate-ClarkeR-20220407.pdf>, accessed 25 May 2023.

Likewise, irregular warfare is about contending narratives, which makes SOF's military information support operations (MISO) relevant, both in shaping perceptions of likely adversaries and addressing disinformation. As SOCOM commander Richard Clarke has testified, SOF is aggressively reorienting its MISO 'to counter strategic competitors' (read: China, Russia, and to lesser degrees Iran and North Korea). A particular focus is information spread online, as evidenced by the recent establishment of a Joint MISO WebOps Center (JMWC).[12] This remains work in progress, and thought is now going into how to incorporate better cyber dimensions into SOF's traditional work on resistance and resilience.[13]

Finally, irregular warfare relates intimately to governance, and so SOF's civil affairs capabilities can play a valuable role in engaging with local populations, identifying political and societal trends, and promoting US interests. Civil Knowledge Integration (CKI), a civil affairs process that integrates societal awareness into planning, could help inform society-wide responses to what some have called 'society-centric warfare'.[14] Much will depend, however, on how well CKI informs the 'leading principals' of such effort, which are unlikely to come from the military.[15] This point speaks to a broader challenge.

The Limits of SOF in Strategic Competition

SOF can contribute in unique ways to strategic competition, but seizing this potential requires understanding SOF's role and its limits. Specifically, as a military force, SOF will always be most relevant where there is an active threat or use of force, hence its natural fit within irregular warfare – a '*violent* struggle for legitimacy'.[16] Strategic competition, however, is only in part about irregular warfare. In most settings, the US's competitors employ 'political warfare', an adjacent but separate term that describes the weaponisation of non-military means to prevail without fighting. As George F Kennan put it in his famous cable of 1946, at the dawn of the Cold War, political warfare is 'the logical application of Clausewitz's doctrine in time of peace'.[17] In practice, political warfare today includes economic pressure, election interference, disinformation, lawfare, intellectual theft, aggressive 'wolf warrior diplomacy', and political infiltration.[18]

Special operations forces can contribute in unique ways to strategic competition

This weaponisation of statecraft mounts an analytical and institutional predicament for the US interagency, which has struggled to adapt in strategically meaningful ways. SOF is often viewed as the problem solver for tasks that cannot be accomplished by others (indeed, a former SOCOM commander defines a 'special operation' as one 'for which no other force is organized, trained and

12. *Ibid*., p. 4.
13. Nicholas A Bredenkamp and Mark Grzegorzewski, 'Supporting Resistance Movements in Cyberspace', *Special Operations Journal* (Vol. 7, No. 1, January 2021), pp. 17–28.
14. See, respectively, Juan Quiroz, 'The Oblique Approach to Irregular Warfare: Civil Affairs as the Main Effort in Strategic Competition', *Small Wars Journal*, 3 January 2023, <https://smallwarsjournal.com/jrnl/art/oblique-approach-irregular-warfare-civil-affairs-main-effort-strategic-competition>, accessed 22 May 2023; Ariel E Levite and Jonathan (Yoni) Shimshoni, 'The Strategic Challenge of Society-Centric Warfare', *Survival* (Vol. 60, No. 6, November 2018), pp. 91–118.
15. Quiroz, 'The Oblique Approach to Irregular Warfare'.
16. This definition has changed in recent years and yet remains, to this author, the most compelling way of framing and distinguishing irregular warfare (emphasis added). For discussion, see David H Ucko and Thomas A Marks, 'Redefining Irregular Warfare: Legitimacy, Coercion, and Power', Modern War Institute, 18 October 2022, <https://mwi.usma.edu/redefining-irregular-warfare-legitimacy-coercion-and-power/>, accessed 22 May 2023. For the original definition, see Department of Defense, 'Irregular Warfare (IW) Joint Operating Concept (JOC)' (Arlington, VA, 11 September 2007), para. 1, p. 3.
17. George F Kennan, 'The Inauguration of Organized Political Warfare [Redacted Version]', 30 April 1948, para. 1, Office of the Historian, US Department of State, <https://history.state.gov/historicaldocuments/frus1945-50Intel/d269>, accessed 22 May 2023.
18. For a discussion of China's embrace of political warfare, which stems back nearly a century, see Thomas A Marks and David H Ucko, 'Gray Zone in Red: China Revisits the Past', *Small Wars & Insurgencies* (Vol. 32, No. 2, 17 February 2021), pp. 181–204.

equipped to conduct').[19] And yet, it is far from clear that these elite forces can or should be relied upon to resolve this particular challenge.

The first consideration relates to SOF's operational tempo, which was too high during the last two decades and caused morale, ethics and recruitment standards to slip.[20] Though the withdrawal from Afghanistan has mitigated this problem, a new normal must be set. Second, the tasks that SOF is expected to master – in particular, FID and unconventional warfare – are so ambitious that they require sustained institutional attention; a focus that should not be diluted by saddling SOF unnecessarily with non-military tasks;[21] in other words, 'just because special forces can conduct a mission does not mean that they should'.[22] Third, while during the War on Terror SOF faced 'just' the challenge of mastering irregular warfare, it must now prepare also for the possibility of large-scale combat operations, all while it also masters integrated deterrence and strategic competition.[23] Fourth, though SOF often promotes its smaller footprint, more efficient use of resources, and quiet and creative ways of solving unorthodox problems, there is nothing inherently low risk about deploying military forces of any type; instead, it can easily cause escalation.[24] Finally, there are other components of the government that have more appropriate authorities and could take on the non-violent lines of effort pursued by state adversaries. Until a comprehensive threat can be met with a comprehensive response, US strategy will lag.

It may be helpful to consider a few examples for which there is no 'SOF easy button'.[25] Corruption and lack of transparency greatly facilitate Chinese efforts at economic and political infiltration, resulting in the subservience of ostensibly sovereign nation states to Chinese interests. The response to this method relies on strengthening the rule of law and in bolstering the 'capacity of independent media, civil society, political parties and private enterprise to force greater transparency'.[26] This effort, so essential to strategic competition, is not an SOF skill. Similarly, Russia seeks to subvert democratic elections, either to discredit the system or to sway outcomes, and there is no clear role for SOF in thwarting this type of attack. SOF also lacks the authority to halt shady investments in the US, or elsewhere, that are likely to affect national security. And what is the likely SOF response to countries

19. Eric T Olson, in Kyle Atwell and Abigail Gage, 'Back to the Future: Resetting Special Operations Forces for Great Power Competition', Irregular Warfare Podcast, <https://mwi.usma.edu/back-to-the-future-resetting-special-operations-forces-for-great-power-competition/>, accessed 22 May 2023.

20. For discussion, see R D Hooker Jr, 'America's Special Operations Problem', *Joint Force Quarterly* (Vol. 108, 1st Quarter, 2023), pp. 51–53. For background, see Andrew Milburn, 'How to Fix a Broken Special Operations Culture', *War on the Rocks*, 13 September 2019; David Martin, 'Navy SEAL Drug Use "Staggering", Investigation Finds', *CBS News*, 11 April 2017; David Choi, 'After Multiple Deployments, US Special Forces May Have "Mortgaged the Future"', *Business Insider*, 3 May 2017.

21. As Schroden argues, 'The desire of US policy-makers to steadily decrease the risk profile of US activities overseas has led to a consistent trend of them asking for SOF to solve their most difficult policy problems, but also increasingly to solve their easy ones, too'. See Jonathan Schroden, 'Why Special Operations? A Risk-Based Theory', CNA, September 2020, p. 33. As Watling adds, 'The political convenience of special operations forces threatens their readiness for tasks where their skills and capabilities are essential enablers for the joint force'. See Jack Watling, 'Old Habits Die Hard: Special Operations Forces, Twenty Years of Counterterrorism, and the New Era of Great Power Competition', *Modern War Institute*, 21 June 2021, <https://mwi.usma.edu/old-habits-die-hard-special-operations-forces-twenty-years-of-counterterrorism-and-the-new-era-of-great-power-competition/>, accessed 22 May 2023.

22. Jack Watling therefore concludes that 'Perhaps the most important prerequisite for special operations forces optimising for great power competition […] is the recognition by policymakers that throwing them into the breach to confront every challenge comes at a cost'. See Watling, 'Old Habits Die Hard'. See also Jack Watling, 'Sharpening the Dagger: Optimising Special Forces for Future Conflict', *Whitehall Report* (London: RUSI, May 2021), p. 19.

23. A point made convincingly by LTG Jonathan Braga, commander of US Army Special Operations Command, in Benjamin Jebb and Kyle Atwell, 'The Cyber-SOF-Space Triad and the Future of Army Special Operations', Irregular Warfare Podcast, 2 May 2023, <https://mwi.usma.edu/irregular-warfare-podcast-the-cyber-sof-space-triad/>, accessed 22 May 2023.

24. This argument runs counter to the popular 'value proposition' of SOF as 'low risk'. For discussion of SOF and risk, see Russell A Burgos, 'Pushing the Easy Button: Special Operations Forces, International Security, and the Use of Force', *Special Operations Journal* (Vol. 4, No. 2, July 2018), pp. 109–28.

25. Brian Dodwell, 'A View from the CT Foxhole: Mark Mitchell, Principal Deputy Assistant Secretary of Defense for Special Operations/Low-Intensity Conflict', *CTC Sentinel* (Vol. 11, No. 11, December 2018), p. 11.

26. David Shullman (ed.), 'Chinese Malign Influence and the Corrosion of Democracy: An Assessment of Chinese Interference in Thirteen Key Countries', International Republican Institute, Washington, DC, 2019, pp. 7–8.

and individuals shirking the sanctions meant to curb hostile behaviour by adversarial states?

These examples are not intended to belittle SOF but to delimit its application in strategic competition. As the US seeks to counter multifaceted strategies, it must look not just or primarily to SOF but to capabilities residing elsewhere. For boosting transparency and combatting corruption, this may involve working through USAID, the State Department and the Department of Justice. The Department of the Treasury has expertise in sanctions enforcement, via its Office of Foreign Assets Control (OFAC), and in tracking illicit financial interactions, via its Financial Crimes and Enforcement Network (FinCEN) and its Office of Terrorism and Financial Intelligence. The recently formed International Development Finance Corporation (DFC) was created specifically as a better alternative to China's Belt and Road Initiative and to facilitate US economic statecraft.[27] In a similar vein, and while primarily domestically focused, the interagency Committee on Foreign Investment in the United States (CFIUS) has expertise in checking dodgy foreign dealings and economic infiltration.[28] To influence foreign audiences, the US can look to the US Agency for Global Media (USAGM), which manages all civilian US international outlets and reaches worldwide audiences of nearly 400 million per week.[29] The Global Engagement Center, while it requires more resources and institutional cachet, also plays a key part in this effort. The list goes on – and could be developed further.

These considerations should also inform how SOF engages in irregular warfare – specifically how it builds resilience and resistance capability abroad. Whereas FID and unconventional warfare are core SOF activities, they seek to resolve a problem that is far more than military. FID is described in doctrine as 'the participation by *civilian agencies and military forces*' to assist another government in countering its domestic threats, and it is meant to nest within that government's 'internal defense and development (IDAD) program', implying interagency-to-interagency engagement throughout.[30] For SOF, the forces it trains must be supported by a capable security sector, girded by sustainable institutions, and operating alongside instruments of state that can take the lead on political, societal and economic matters. Producing such synergy is anything but easy. Indeed, the failure to engage comprehensively in this manner has been a major drag on past advisory efforts.[31]

In unconventional warfare, the tasks undertaken by security forces and armed units must be complemented ideally by a whole-of-society effort

Similarly, in unconventional warfare, or in fostering resistance, the tasks undertaken by security forces and armed units must be complemented ideally by a whole-of-society effort. As Fiala argues, it may require a Ministry of Justice effort to help create the legal construct for resistance organisations, a Ministry of Foreign Affairs effort to engage with allies and partners for support and recognition, a Ministry of Communication effort to build a narrative for mobilisation domestically and abroad, a Ministry of Education or of Culture to develop national pride and confidence, and various civil society organisations to champion these goals

27. Shayerah I Akhtar and Nick M Brown, 'U.S. International Development Finance Corporation: Overview and Issues', CRS Report for Congress (Washington, DC: Congressional Research Service, 10 January 2022); Daniel Kliman, 'Leverage the New US International Development Finance Corporation to Compete with China', *The Hill*, 16 November 2018, <https://thehill.com/opinion/international/416904-leverage-us-international-development-finance-corporation-compete-with-china/>, accessed 24 May 2023.
28. Kevin Granville, 'Cfius, Powerful and Unseen, is a Gatekeeper on Major Deals', *New York Times*, 5 March 2018.
29. Sim Farar, William J Hybl and Anne Wedner, '2022 Comprehensive Annual Report on Public Diplomacy and International Broadcasting', Focus on FY 21 Budget Data, 2022, pp. 195–96, <https://www.state.gov/wp-content/uploads/2022/12/FINAL_2022_ACPD_AnnualReport_508Ready.pdf>, accessed 22 May 2023.
30. Joint Chiefs of Staff, 'Joint Publication 3-22, Foreign Internal Defense' (Arlington, VA: Department of Defense, 17 August 2018), p. ix I—1 (emphasis added).
31. Brian M Burton, 'The Promise and Peril of the Indirect Approach', *PRISM* (Vol. 3, No. 1, 2011), pp. 53–57. Witness equally the superb performance of Iraq's special operations unit in the face of ISIS, in contrast to the faltering of its conventional military and the crippling, and far more intractable, weaknesses of its political institutions.

and carry them to the populace.[32] The ongoing support to Ukraine underlines these requirements, as well as the foundational importance of counter-corruption and, more broadly, legitimacy.[33]

As SOF establishes its remit in boosting resilience and resistance, it must be careful not to veer into civilian realms where other agencies should lead. Some have suggested, for example, as SOF priorities, 'cognitive access denial' or 'financial access denial', to wit, resisting propaganda and disrupting 'proxy, patronage, or corruption networks'.[34] These tasks are important, but it is unclear whether SOF is educated, trained or mandated to handle their complexity. Susceptibility to disinformation, for example, speaks to economic precariousness, political marginalisation, media monopolies, and – ultimately – questions of legitimacy. Countering threat finance requires financial intelligence, anti-money laundering capabilities, and an understanding of the illicit and licit international political economy. These are not matters that special operations forces should manage. Even where SOF has relevant capability – for example its MISO assets – so do other instruments of power, be it within the Department of State, the USAGM, and within the country teams.[35] Meanwhile, SOF is meant to bring something special, and specialise in that area.

Ways Forward: Integration and Support

The primarily non-military nature of strategic competition does not make SOF irrelevant. It does mean, however, that in defining its role, SOF will need to think of itself, present itself, and be used to empower an interagency solution. SOF's indispensable contribution should be to add that special ingredient that allows a broader response to unfold. This type of role often comes naturally to the SOF community, given its emphasis on partnerships, but it rubs up against its desire to carve out unique relevance in a new strategic era and its occasional (and by no means universal) tendency to operate in parallel rather than in support of civilian government agencies.[36] Ultimately, however, it is an approach that would not only boost US competitiveness but also allow SOF to contribute less often but in more impactful ways, thereby sustaining a manageable operational tempo.

The primarily non-military nature of strategic competition does not make special operations forces irrelevant

There is ample precedent for these types of supportive arrangements. As commander of Special Operations Command Pacific (SOCPAC), General Jonathan P Braga oversaw an impressive operational effort to counter Chinese malign influence in Southeast Asia and the Pacific Islands. Through partnerships with Treasury, the FBI, and the Department of Justice at US Indo-Pacific Command (INDOPACOM), a small SOCPAC team was able to recover and analyse evidence relating to Chinese Communist Party (CCP)-linked criminal networks, resulting in the Office of Foreign Assets Control

32. Otto C Fiala, 'Resistance Resurgent: Resurrecting a Method of Irregular Warfare in Great Power Competition', *Special Operations Journal* (Vol. 7, No. 2, July 2021), p. 124.
33. On this point, some experts on proxy war decry the 'chronic failures' of the US 'to consider ethnography, legitimacy, and long-term effects of proxy sponsorship on regional security and stability'. See Claire Graja, 'SOF and the Future of Global Competition', CNA Conference Proceedings, Arlington, May 2019, p. 5.
34. Katie Crombe, Steve Ferenzi and Robert Jones, 'Integrating Deterrence across the Gray – Making It More than Words', *Military Times*, 9 December 2021, <https://www.militarytimes.com/opinion/commentary/2021/12/08/integrating-deterrence-across-the-gray-making-it-more-than-words/>, accessed 22 May 2023. See also Bryan Groves and Steve Ferenzi, 'Unconventional Deterrence in Europe: The Role of Army Special Operations in Competition Today', *RealClearDefense*, 16 April 2020, <https://www.realcleardefense.com/articles/2020/04/16/unconventional_deterrence_in_europe_the_role_of_army_special_operations_in_competition_today_115207.html>, accessed 22 May 2023.
35. For a full account of US government assets for countering disinformation, see Jesse S Curtis, 'Springing the "Tacitus Trap": Countering Chinese State-Sponsored Disinformation', *Small Wars and Insurgencies* (Vol. 32, No. 2, 17 February 2021), Fig. 3.
36. For discussion of this tendency, in relation to 127e authorities (to arm, train, and empower foreign forces to conduct US-directed missions), see Nick Turse and Alice Speri, 'How the Pentagon Uses a Secretive Program to Wage Proxy Wars', *The Intercept*, 1 July 2022, <https://theintercept.com/2022/07/01/pentagon-127e-proxy-wars/>, accessed 22 May 2023. For the broader issue of SOF mis- and overuse, see Alice Friend and Shannon Culbertson, 'Special Obfuscations: The Strategic Uses of Special Operations Forces', CSIS Briefs, Washington, DC, March 2020.

(OFAC) sanctioning Wan Kuok-koi ('Broken Tooth') and his network under the Global Magnitsky Act.[37] The CCP has a track record of using criminal proxies to undermine states in the region.[38] By acting via the intelligence community and its own analysts, SOF empowered the necessary agencies to respond to this non-military approach. In a similar manner, SOCPAC has worked with the Department of Commerce's National Oceanic and Atmospheric Administration (NOAA) to investigate, report on, and check the Chinese fishing companies operating illegally in the South Pacific. Through MISO, SOCPAC was able to broadcast the horrific images that accompany this activity to senior INDOPACOM, Coast Guard, State Department, and other Washington advisors and decision makers.[39]

Unsurprisingly, this need for integration also concerns SOF's work alongside general-purpose forces. According to some measures, SOF comprises just 2% of the joint force. While the return on this investment is often celebrated, it does not come without cost.[40] The limits of the possible are now accentuated by the need for SOF to combine counterterrorism and strategic competition priorities, not to mention preparing for a possible war, all with shrinking resources.[41] Thus, the US Army's belated creation of Security Force Assistance Brigades in 2017 was a necessary step in the right direction. Through a further partnership with the National Guard's State Partnership Program, it should be possible to divide labour in a manner that allows SOF to specialise and contribute specifically when it is needed.[42] Even in those contexts, of course, focusing just on elite forces is insufficient, and so SOF efforts will always require nesting within a broader engagement.[43]

Detractors to this type of burden-sharing will point out that neither the general-purpose forces nor the interagency have the capacity and/or capability to engage effectively with the irregular and asymmetric activities undertaken by SOF. This point has merit. Within the military, this calls for a more concerted focus on irregular warfare, something that the general-purpose forces have typically resisted.[44]

---

37. US Department of the Treasury, 'Treasury Sanctions Corrupt Actors in Africa and Asia', press release, 9 December 2020, <https://home.treasury.gov/news/press-releases/sm1206>, accessed 22 May 2023. For discussion of how sanctions could more effectively be integrated as a component of deterrence and signalling, see Elizabeth Rosenberg and Jordan Tama, 'Strengthening the Economic Arsenal: Bolstering the Deterrent and Signaling Effects of Sanctions', Center for a New American Security, Washington, DC, December 2019.
38. Michael J Cole, 'On the Role of Organized Crime and Related Substate Actors in Chinese Political Warfare Against Taiwan', *Prospects & Exploration* (Vol. 19, No. 6, 2021), pp. 55–88.
39. For context, see Matthew West, 'Coast Guard Releases New Plan to Combat Illegal, Unreported, and Unregulated Fishing World', US Indo-Pacific Command, 18 September 2020.
40. United States Government Accountability Office, 'Special Operations Forces: Better Data Necessary to Improve Oversight and Address Command and Control Challenges', Report to Congressional Committees (Washington, DC, October 2022). For a critique on the return on investment, see Hooker, 'America's Special Operations Problem'.
41. In 2021, General Richard D Clarke, then the USSOCOM Commander, testified that: 'Our deployed forces are down 15% from last year – the lowest since 2001, and in FY21, nearly 40% of our deployed forces will focus on GPC requirements'. Special Operations Command, 'Posture Statement of General Richard D Clarke, USA, Commander, United States Special Operations Command before the 117th Congress House Committee on Appropriations Subcommittee on Defense', Washington DC, March 2021, p. 4.
42. For a revealing glimpse into the tensions within SOF created by the SFAB, see Tim Ball, 'Replaced? Security Force Assistance Brigades vs. Special Forces', *War on the Rocks*, 23 February 2017. For a proposal of how these security force assistance efforts can work together, see Charles McEnany, 'The US Army's Security Force Assistance Triad: Security Force Assistance Brigades, Special Forces and the State Partnership Program', Association of the United States Army, 3 October 2022, <http://www.ausa.org/publications/us-armys-security-force-assistance-triad-security-force-assistance-brigades-special>, accessed 22 May 2023.
43. Tommy Ross and Philip McDaniel, 'Training Law Enforcement in Fragile States: The Case for a New US Approach', *War on the Rocks*, 25 March 2019. As Michael Vickers has also argued, 'Security forces are part of society [...] One of my complaints about SOF is that SOF would only want to partner with the commando or counter-terror [CT] units. So, they end up training one incredible CT unit, but you don't win wars with that'. John Taft, Liz Gorminsky and Joe Mariani, 'Special Operations Forces and Great Power Competition: Talent, Technology, and Organizational Change in the New Threat Environment', Deloitte Insights, 2019, p. 11, <https://www2.deloitte.com/content/dam/insights/us/articles/4980_special-operations-forces/DI_special-operations-forces.pdf>, accessed 25 May 2023.
44. One may point to the need for an Irregular Warfare annex in the 2018 National Defense Strategy, to institutionalise the related capabilities, but also to the stifling difficulties in implementing its recommendations, and to the disappearance

Beyond the military, the problem is compounded by a lack of any real culture for organised, troops-to-task planning for strategic competition. Accordingly, the Department of Defense's recent Joint Concept for Competing emphasised the need to 'expand the competitive mindset' and 'advance integrated campaigning' across the US national security enterprise (an enterprise that now extends far beyond the traditional security sector).[45]

Pending greater reform in this area, it will behove military commanders, within the special operations community and beyond, to use their resources and culture to enable and empower the right partners for the right mission. Not only is such burden-sharing and integration a more efficient use of resources, and a necessary source of support for a relatively small special operations force, but it also reflects the fact that strategic competition, or irregular warfare for that matter, cannot be quarantined within the SOF community in the hope of not upsetting programmes and priorities elsewhere.[46] We all operate in the human domain – the one that SOF calls its home – and we best prepare accordingly.

Pending greater reform in this area, it will behove military commanders, within the special operations community and beyond, to use their resources and culture to enable and empower the right partners for the right mission

Conclusion and Recommendations

Following key roles in fighting Al-Qa'ida and Islamic State, the special operations community is making its case for relevance in a new era of strategic competition. Based on its competence with FID, SOF can assist partners and allies threatened by state-sponsored subversion. Based on its experience with unconventional warfare, it can boost partners' capability to resist or deter foreign occupation. Its competence with civil affairs and information operations is also valuable for a competition driven by societal penetration and contending narratives. Going further, SOF's global engagement and presence help develop the trust and partnerships necessary to mount a common front against revisionist states.

SOF clearly has the potential to contribute to the strategic competition underway and yet its role needs to be carefully understood so that it is neither downplayed nor allowed to dominate in areas where other agencies are a more natural fit. Strategic competition is primarily a non-violent effort, as China and Russia strive to avoid US military strengths and strike instead via societal, political and economic lines of effort. It follows that SOF cannot and should not be expected to carry the load by itself. Against this, however, political leaders often look to SOF for seemingly low-risk and small-footprint solutions to unorthodox problems. As SOF is accustomed to fighting for equities and profile, it also risks overselling its services. There is, therefore, a real danger of SOF being handed ever more missions – missions for which it is not ready and for which it cannot prepare without accepting risk elsewhere – all while the broader portfolio of interagency capabilities remains underfunded and underused.

The key priority for SOF going forward will be to institutionalise the capabilities needed to build resilience and resistance against state-sponsored subversion, insurgency and proxy warfare. Already in these core competences, SOF is expected to master a range of extremely important and equally complex missions. The challenge is indeed significant, given the erosion of capability during the last two decades of direct-action counterterrorism, the need to reorient FID and unconventional warfare for a new strategic era, and for SOF also to remain seized should irregular warfare give way to large-scale combat operations. Given these demands, SOF should desist from taking on primarily non-military duties and tasks, and instead look to support other players for these essential components of strategic competition. Through such synergy, and when nested within a strategic plan, the US can compete – even prevail.

of IW altogether in the subsequent NDS. See David H Ucko, 'Nobody Puts IW in an Annex: It's Time to Embrace Irregular Warfare as a Strategic Priority', *Modern War Institute*, 14 October 2020, <https://mwi.usma.edu/nobody-puts-iw-in-an-annex-its-time-to-embrace-irregular-warfare-as-a-strategic-priority/>, accessed 22 May 2023.

45. See Department of Defense, Joint Chiefs of Staff, 'Joint Concept for Competing', 10 February 2023, p. 37.
46. For one proposal, see Phillip Lohaus, 'Special Operations Forces in the Gray Zone: An Operational Framework for Using Special Operations Forces in the Space Between War and Peace', *Special Operations Journal* (Vol. 2, No. 2, July 2016), pp. 75–91.

This analysis points to three recommendations.

1. Build Irregular Warfare Awareness

Efforts should be made to maximise irregular warfare training and education for SOF – and for those partners alongside which it will operate. Combined senior-service education that brings together personnel from all relevant institutions would help build government-wide awareness of the irregular warfare challenge and of respective options for response. The College of International Security Affairs (CISA) at the National Defense University provides promising models that could be scaled up for greater effect. At Fort McNair, Washington, DC, it operates under a specific security cooperation programme to provide irregular warfare education and training to senior officials from across the armed services, the intelligence community, the interagency and partner nations.[47] At its programme at Fort Bragg, civilian academics teach a Master's curriculum focused on irregular warfare to US (mostly army special operations forces) officers and NCOs, alongside international SOF students and State Department foreign service officers and diplomatic security personnel. Both programmes could be expanded, if resourced appropriately, to encourage more cultural and organisational integration for the challenge at hand.

2. Enhance and Integrate Civilian Capability for Competition

The civilian agencies best placed to counter hostile non-military lines of effort require broader funding, capacity and mandates. A first step is to generate a 'competitive mindset' in institutions too often isolated from national security discussions. From then on, cross-functional teams, liaison officers, and other structural ways of cutting across agencies may help bring common awareness of respective strengths and authorities, and thereby enable integration in practice. Despite funding inequities between military and non-military bodies, there are promising precedents, ranging from Operation *Warp Speed* (the US's development of the first Covid-19 vaccines), the Defeat-ISIS Task Force, Embassy Country Teams, and Joint Interagency Task Forces. As seen, theatre special operations commands such as SOCPAC have also succeeded in cobbling together their own interagency fusion teams. Such practices must be studied, replicated and institutionalised.

3. Strategic Clarity

An aware, capable, joint and interagency force still requires strategic direction to meet specific ends in line with policy. The 'Joint Concept for Competing' puts it well: 'Countering an adversary's competitive strategies is not as simple or straightforward as just blocking or challenging the adversary wherever it seeks to act'.[48] Instead, the ultimate requirement is for a strategy that proceeds according to a compelling theory of success.[49] It is not clear who currently sets this strategy, what the US is competing for, what its core interests are, and how it may define success. Strategic ambiguity certainly has value, but it should confound America's adversaries, not itself. ■

David H Ucko is professor at the College of International Security Affairs (CISA), National Defense University. His most recent works include *The Insurgent's Dilemma: A Struggle to Prevail* (Hurst/OUP, 2022) and, with Thomas A Marks, *Crafting Strategy for Irregular Warfare: A Framework for Analysis and Action*, 2nd ed. (NDU Press, 2022).

The views presented are those of the author and do not necessarily represent the views of the Department of Defense or its components. This article is based on testimony provided by the author to the Intelligence and Special Operations Subcommittee of the US House of Representatives' Armed Services Committee on 8 February 2023.

47. This programme is the Regional Defense Combating Terrorism and Irregular Warfare Fellowship Program, codified in section 345 of the National Defense Authorization Act.
48. Joint Chiefs of Staff, 'Joint Concept for Competing', p. 28.
49. On the crucial strategic requirement for a theory of victory, or at least of success, see Frank G Hoffman, 'The Missing Element in Crafting National Strategy: A Theory of Success', *Joint Force Quarterly* (Vol. 97, 2nd Quarter, 2020) and Jeffrey W Meiser, 'Ends + Ways + Means = (Bad) Strategy', *Parameters* (Vol. 46, No. 4, 2016), pp. 81–91.

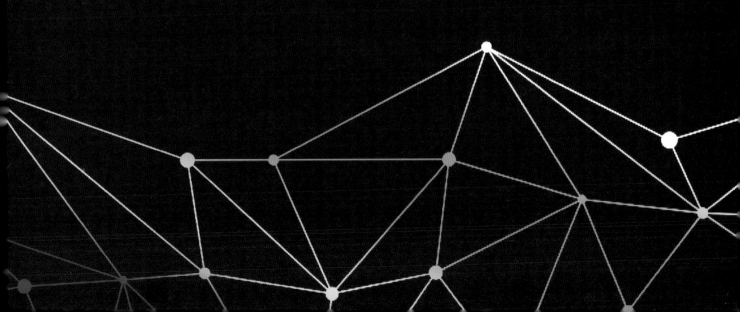

The Future Commando Force

A Tactical Dilemma

James White

Planners of the new Future Commando Force concept envisage small, highly versatile teams, attacking key enemy targets. This concept of disaggregated infiltration tactics means it is essential every Royal Marine is trained to an excellent level. James White provides a study of warfighting operations from a close-combat perspective and argues that whilst the Royal Marines has an exceptionally strong moral component, its conceptual component – specifically at this lower tactical level – is often poor. There is a direct correlation between the way in which the Royal Marines are organised and shallow tactical understanding.

The new Future Commando Force (FCF) concept shapes the Royal Marines into an expeditionary raiding force. It is designed to fight high intensity warfare, against peer or near-peer adversaries. Forward deployed and supported by a variety of Royal Navy platforms, the force is scaleable and highly versatile, ensuring it can escalate through a range of threats. The FCF plan is ambitious, bold and innovative; yet it has a critical flaw.

Deep within the physical component of the FCF model, the Royal Marines' approach to its force design has a subsequent, detrimental effect on close-combat proficiency. This heavily influences training, readiness and conceptual understanding.

Context

Accuracy

As military academics consider the potential of the FCF, focus is naturally placed on the higher strategic and operational levels of war. To ensure analysis and subsequent conclusions are accurate, it is important to include the basic, visceral details of conflict. This lower tactical level has a significant effect on overall understanding and it is essential to consider, because this is the point at which combat takes place. 'The level of which the battle is won, as it always will be won or lost, is at the company, platoon and section level'.[1] This is the point at which violence is applied, or violence is at least threatened.

The following essay is therefore a study of the FCF from a close-combat perspective. Its aim is to document an enduring, fiercely critical observation of the Royal Marines' ability to conduct tactical level warfighting operations. Its central message argues that whilst the Royal Marines has an exceptionally strong moral component, its conceptual component – specifically at this lower tactical level – is often poor. There is a direct correlation between the way in which the Royal Marines is organised and shallow tactical understanding.

Lineage

The Royal Marines is a historic, storied regiment. It has a lineage of institutionalised success and is considered among the best units within the UK armed forces. Today it forms an amphibious, elite infantry.

1. Colonel Dumphie MC, 'Falklands War: The Land Battle Part 4 - In the Light of Experience', <https://m.youtube.com/watch?v=m1uH1YnFvgk>, accessed 17 March 2023.

© RUSI Journal, Vol. 168, No. 3, 2023 pp. 22–30

Royal Marines from Yankee Company on a mountain march in the Slovenian mountains, 2022. *Courtesy of Ministry of Defence / Kevin Walton / Crown Copyright / OGL 3.0*

Its central manoeuvre formation, the highly regarded 3 Commando Brigade, is used as a rapid reaction force – the vanguard of the UK government's intervention operations. The Royal Marines is also responsible for a wide range of broader tasks, such as the protection of the UK's nuclear deterrent and maritime security.

In November 2019, a paper by Sidhart Kaushal and Jack Watling identified two trends that define the modern character of amphibious assault.[2] The first is the growing importance of coastal, urban areas; meaning the littoral has now become the strategic centre of gravity. Amphibious operations against coastal targets are therefore becoming increasingly important. The second is the difficulty of approaching these littoral areas in order to conduct amphibious assault. The paper states: 'Maturation of precision-strike capabilities and ISR systems that enable them, along with the proliferation of technology associated with the concept of anti-access area denial (A2AD), will make traditional amphibious assaults and ship to objective manoeuvres ever-more difficult'.[3]

In addition, following the publication of the Integrated Review,[4] the army announced the formation of a four-battalion Ranger Regiment, the main component of a new Special Operations Brigade. Then Chief of the General Staff, General Sir Mark Carleton-Smith, stated: 'The Army Special Operations Brigade is designed to operate alongside both regular, irregular and proxies in high threat, hostile environments'.[5] With huge emphasis and investment placed on the new formation by the army, this was perceived as direct inter-service competition – a threat to employment and tasks, traditionally the preserve of the Commandos.

To shape its force to operate effectively in the new strategic environment and to maintain competitive advantage within Defence, the Royal Marines had to evolve – as then Secretary of State for Defence Gavin Williamson pointed out in February 2019, when he 'announced that the Royal Navy would be investing in the development of, and experimentation with,

2. Sidharth Kaushal and Jack Watling, 'Requirements for the UK's Amphibious Forces in the Future Operating Environment', *RUSI Occasional Papers* (November 2019).
3. *Ibid.*, p. 10.
4. Ministry of Defence, 'Army Announces Special Ops Army Ranger Regiment', 23 March 2021, <https://www.gov.uk/government/news/army-announces-special-ops-army-ranger-regiment>, accessed 17 March 2023.
5. *Ibid.*

a littoral strike concept to lay the operational requirements for a Future Commando Force'.[6]

The Corps of Specialists

The process used to generate manning for the Royal Marines force structure is termed the Corps of Specialists ((RM)CoS) approach. Expressed in its simplest terms, the force is enabled by a 'core of Specialist' Commandos.[7] In the British Army Regimental system, Combat Service Support (CSS) and Combat Support (CS) units provide direct support to the infantry combat force. Comparably, in the Royal Marines, they are also responsible for the conduct of the infantry role. Essentially, there is no dedicated infantry, or what contemporary doctrine terms Dismounted Close-Combat (DCC). Specialisations that are considered support roles, such as clerk, driver or engineer, simply rotate through the infantry positions.

Royal Marines recruit training is based on the infantry syllabus and achieves the DCC qualification. The iconic Commando tests are added to this core programme, building Royal Marines training into a 33-week course; the longest, and arguably hardest, basic training in the military.

On successful completion, every rank within the Royal Marines will train in a Primary Specialist Qualification (PSQ) at some point early in their career. These are taken from a range of CSS or CS disciplines. These specialisations are then required to act, intermittently, as infantry. There is also a requirement to train in multiple Secondary Specialist Qualifications (SSQ); additional short courses that provide enabling skills, such as team level logistician or medic. This system is applied throughout the lower levels of tactical command, for example, the Regimental Sergeant Major who led 42 Commando during the 2003 invasion of Iraq, specialised as a clerk. As an isolated, amphibious infantry unit under Royal Navy command, this concept is unique to the Royal Marines. The approach is designed to ensure the Royal Marines is self-sufficient; independent from the mass of army infantry units and able to operate autonomously within the armed forces.

In an era of constant force reduction, in which some of the army's most celebrated regiments have been amalgamated and some entirely disbanded, the Strategic Defence Reviews had become an existential threat. The (RM)CoS approach allows the Royal Marines to provide the UK government and wider Defence with a perception of utility and value. The approach also offers flexibility, enabling this self-sufficient, highly trained organisation to 'change rapidly, appropriately and effectively to new circumstances'.[8] The theoretical basis of this approach is that once Commando trained, every rank is able to rotate through the different aspects of combat.

However, the (RM)CoS has deeply engrained errors. These are inherent in the approach and detrimental to the Royal Marines' tactical ability. As Royal Marines ranks, including tactical level commanders, rotate through their specialisations and DCC role, infantry training is constantly disrupted; over time the effect becomes significant. Through this design, the Royal Marines has developed a system that claims several important advantages but hinders the primary function of a close-combat unit.

The Tactical Setting

Sub-culture

This approach leads to an obvious difference in culture between the British Army infantry and the Royal Marines. The infantry exist in a culture of platoon tactics; it is profoundly important to both their character and self-esteem. The image of the combat infantryman creates an expectation that defines their central identity.

In the Royal Marines, the myriad of specialisations appears to blur this singularity. Instead, both physical training and the 'Commando ethos' seem to become the unifying characteristics. Physical training has a disproportionate importance; a 'mock primacy'. Prominent in their culture from recruit training, the Commando tests engrain physical pride in the Royal Marines psyche. This is underpinned by the highest moral standards and fierce confidence. Royal Marines culture is outlined by physical excellence, the ability to adapt and exemplary moral standards – symbolised by the coveted Green Beret.

6. Kaushal and Watling, 'Requirements for the UK's Amphibious Forces in the Future Operating Environment', p. 2.
7. Ministry of Defence, 'Royal Marines Career Handbook', 2015 edition, p. 2, <https://www.whatdotheyknow.com/request/478172/response/1274939/attach/3/RM%20Career%20Handbook%20Redacted%20001.pdf?cookie_passthrough=1>, accessed 23 May 2023.
8. Army Doctrine Publication AC71940, 'Land Operations. Annex1A, Principles of War, 1A-3'.

Enabling Support

The regimental system is the schematic used to organise most combat forces. This generic blueprint ensures capability is balanced in the most effective way. The (RM)CoS differs and is unique amongst any equivalent unit. The nature of amphibious assault means 3 Commando Brigade must include all of the elements needed to conduct littoral operations, such as: reconnaissance, engineers, artillery and logistical support. The Brigade is defined as a 'self-contained expeditionary force'.[9] The origins of the (RM)CoS concept lies in this requirement. Its key function is to allow the organisation to be self-sufficient, enabling a flexible, dynamic approach to warfighting.

However, if a realistic tactical setting is considered, it is most probable that the Royal Marines will be deployed within a modern, complex battlegroup in future operations. The FCF will most likely operate as a manoeuvre element within a Combined Joint Task Force, involving multi-agency, multi-national and NATO forces.

Even in an amphibious operation conducted entirely by UK forces, the Royal Marines will never be used in isolation. Ivar Hellberg was the Commanding Officer of the Commando Logistic Regiment during the Falklands campaign in 1982. His account of Operation *Corporate* shows an operational order, which illustrates the variety of units used to build 3 Commando Brigade into a divisional size force. Supporting regiments include the Scots Guards 2nd Battalion, the Welsh Guards 1st Battalion, the 63 Squadron RAF (Rapier) and the 518 Company Royal Pioneer Corps.[10]

Even in an amphibious operation conducted entirely by UK forces, the Royal Marines will never be used in isolation

Recent campaigns in Afghanistan and Iraq show that from the company group to corps level, at every point of examination, all Royal Marines actions were supported by other arms or partner forces. An honest acknowledgement of this broad support, used to augment Combat Service Support PSQs, will allow the Royal Marines to streamline roles. FCF teams will then be able to include a dedicated DCC component.

Tactical Nature

Aim

The British Army's capstone doctrine, ADP Land Operations, states the following: 'Principles of War provide comprehensive considerations at all levels for planning and executing campaigns and operations. [Principles] provide a foundation for adversary-focused military activity and doctrine'. It then states: 'the selection and maintenance of aim is the "master" principle of War'.[11]

To set this study in context and provide a clear understanding, it is necessary to define the nature of the FCF and articulate its aim. However much it differs from the army due to its amphibious character and the wide range of specialised tasks it conducts, the central role of the Royal Marines is to conduct infantry combat. To extract the fundamental aim amidst the multiplicity of Royal Marines tactical roles, one must start by illustrating the infantry mission: 'to defeat the enemy in close-combat'.[12] The essential way in which infantry achieve this is by applying fire effect, principally with small-arms, to 'incapacitate or suppress'[13] enemy forces. The single, unambiguous aim of infantry tactical fighting and, therefore, the FCF, is to defeat enemy forces with marksmanship, using supporting tactics and skills such as fieldcraft to maximise lethality.

Specificity

Close combat is the most dangerous aspect of war fighting; it carries the highest risk and demands

9. UK Parliament, 'Sunset for the Royal Marines? The Royal Marines and UK Amphibious Capability', Defence Committee Publications, 1 February 2018, <https://publications.parliament.uk/pa/cm201719/cmselect/cmdfence/622/62207.htm>, accessed 17 March 2023.
10. Ivar Hellberg, 'Falklands Logistics: A Reflection on an Ultimate Challenge 40 Years On', *RUSI Journal* (Vol. 167, No. 1, 2022).
11. Army Doctrine Publication AC71940, 'Land Operations. Annex1A, Principles of War, 1A-1', p. 12, <https://assets.publishing.service.gov.uk/government/uploads/system/uploads/attachment_data/file/605298/Army_Field_Manual__AFM__A5_Master_ADP_Interactive_Gov_Web.pdf>, accessed 23 May 2023.
12. British Army, 'Who We Are', <https://www.army.mod.uk/who-we-are/corps-regiments-and-units/infantry/>, accessed 23 May 2023.
13. Jim Storr, 'High Explosive: Shock Effect in Dismounted Combat', *RUSI Defence Systems*, February 2010, p. 56.

versed infantry skill to be successful. Years of thorough study and experience are needed to be truly competent. The army's regimental system has a dedicated DCC role. This guarantees specificity, allowing the infantry to focus entirely on close combat throughout their careers. Comparably, the Royal Marines approach requires different specialisations to rotate through the DCC positions, before they then return to their original trades.[14] As individuals only spend brief, transient periods practising close combat, this process is naturally disruptive to its development. Opportunities to study and gain experience in infantry tactics are fleeting, and aptitude for its conduct fades, as emphasis gradually shifts to respective specialisations.

Isolating a single, narrow role ensures a thorough knowledge of the subject. Training for combat should always be based on specificity; repeatedly practised, pressure tested and then performance analysed. This is a universal process, which guarantees the subject is understood with a muscular depth, the practitioner has the necessary level of ability and cohesive teams can achieve tactical success. Specificity is a scientific law in achieving high performance; yet by its own design, the Royal Marines splinters the manner in which it practices close combat. It is not sufficient to train in a supporting specialisation, then intermittently conduct the fighting role and, more importantly, take command in that role. Considering the DCC role as a specialisation must have primacy.

Training for combat should always be based on specificity; repeatedly practised, pressure tested and then performance analysed

All ranks are expected to train in a PSQ and up to four SSQ. Rotating between these roles and with a list of divergent, complex skills, means specificity is immediately lost. 'We can't do everything well',[15] and, in aligning to conduct warfighting operations, the FCF must demonstrate 'ruthless prioritisation'.[16]

Performance

Certainty

Capstone doctrine has been used to precisely define the aim of the DCC role. To understand how the (RM) CoS influences tactical performance, it is necessary to refine this core aim in more detail. The ability of the FCF in close combat can then be measured.

Infantry sections close with and defeat enemy forces, principally with the use of small-arms marksmanship, enabling this lethal effect with tactics, battle-drills and fieldcraft. This must be the preeminent factor when considering the FCF teams' effectiveness.

The personnel used to conduct the DCC role in the Royal Marines, and in turn, future FCF operations, are Marines, most having only recently passed basic training, or who come from a variety of different support backgrounds. They are commanded entirely by leadership from these supporting specialisations.

To analyse whether this is the best approach to prepare for the violent pressure test of combat, the following two examples compare Royal Marines and army infantry in direct competition. They are used here to test the key skills of marksmanship and the application of tactics: both prove instructive.

Precision Lethality

Post operational reports consistently state that artillery and supporting fires account for the majority of enemy casualties. Yet, in close-combat fighting, it is effective small-arms fire which incapacitates and suppresses enemy forces: 'for the platoon, combat effectiveness relies on the application of effective firepower'.[17]

Therefore, in an infantry unit, it is accurate marksmanship that is considered the most important skill: 'At the level of minor tactics, accurate firepower is the key to combat performance'.[18]

The Defence Operational Shooting Competition (DefOSC) is a long-established, major event, conducted at the National Shooting Centre, Bisley. In this annual marksmanship competition, teams compete for a series of trophies and events; culminating in the prestigious Queen's Medal Award and inter-service rifle match. The matches simulate

14. Each 'Draft' cycle is usually a two-year assignment.
15. Patrick Sanders, 'Keynote Speech', proceedings of the RUSI Land Warfare conference, London, UK, 28 June 2022.
16. *Ibid.*
17. Anthony King, *The Combat Soldier, Infantry Tactics and Cohesion in the Twentieth and Twenty-First Centuries* (Oxford: Oxford University Press, 2013), p. 38.
18. *Ibid.*

realistic battle conditions, involving physical movement, moving targets and long-range rifle fire; it is a test of marksmanship in a pure form.

On the final day of competition, the Royal Marines and army directly compete in the inter-service rifle match. This defining event is routinely won by the army shooting team and rarely awarded to the Royal Marines. The match is used here as an objective test of combat marksmanship, in which the army infantry teams repeatedly beat Royal Marines teams.

Attacks

British Army Training Unit Kenya (BATUK) provides the light infantry testing area. Infantry battalions conduct live fire tactical training (LFTT) and are subsequently graded on their combat performance. The Royal Marines has no equivalent: there is no validated testing of the DCC component within the Royal Marines. There are formal test standards when training in specialisations; additionally, there are short assessments of command on promotional courses and practice periods on training exercises. However, there is no formal grading by independent assessors for Royal Marines close-combat units, as infantry forces have in BATUK.

Without this means of testing the (RM)CoS in relation to infantry fighting, the Royal Marines command relies on a number of rudimentary factors as assurance of tactical ability: all ranks will have passed basic training, and commanders will have passed a short DCC assessment on their promotional course; and most have trained in a supporting role, some as vividly distinct from infantry tactics as drill instructor and vehicle mechanic.

Operating in isolation within the Royal Navy, away from the mass of army regiments and wider UK land forces, it is difficult to compare the Royal Marines with equivalent units. A contentious exercise in 2007 informs the point. As the embryonic Special Forces Support Group was being developed, a series of LFTT tests were conducted to evaluate close-combat proficiency. The initial Royal Marines personnel directed to fill this infantry role were fiercely criticised. Directing staff were acutely negative of the Royal Marines' performance, flaring rivalries and venomous argument. At the time, this was attributed as regimental bias but, as a marker of Royal Marines tactical ability, these tests proved insightful. Specialists such as drivers and physical-training instructors, had little or no time to practise together, often using crude frontal attacks in the assault.[19] In contrast, the 1PARA sections and platoons achieved higher performance standards, having worked together consistently in small teams, collectively practising infantry tactics. The results of these tests were largely ignored by the Royal Marines command responsible for infantry training at that time, yet the results are prescient for FCF performance.

From this narrow perspective of close combat, when placed in direct competition, there is a marked difference in performance between the Royal Marines and army infantry sections.

Atrophy

The Royal Marines arguably recruits the best personnel in Defence, routinely attracting individuals of the highest educational standards. From the outset of their basic training, the Royal Marines engrains an outstanding professional ethos. Its instructors are passionate, motivated and articulate. Conversely, in tactical ability and conceptual understanding, the Royal Marines fails to realise this vast potential. It is this (RM)CoS design which has an immediate and enduring effect on training and the adeptness of close combat.

The Royal Marines arguably recruit the best personnel in Defence, routinely attracting individuals of the highest educational standards

The different Royal Marines specialisations are used to teach close-combat throughout recruit training. This is augmented by specialists teaching in their own roles, such as mountain leaders and communicators teaching vertical assault and signalling respectively. Infantry platoon tactics, marksmanship and fieldcraft are taught by instructors that have only intermittently conducted the DCC role, often with limited experience.

On successful completion of basic training, the (RM)CoS continues to influence understanding as individuals progress to Commando units. The tempo and volume of unit commitments appears exhaustive. Shallow annual tests and mandatory lectures take up further time. As preparation for the broad range of specialised Royal Marines tasks is directed and prioritised, ensuring a balanced

19. Author interview with Small-arms School Corps (SASC) directing staff conducting the LFTT exercise, 2008, and follow-up conversations. The SASC advises and instructs infantry on weapon systems and range management.

approach to training becomes strained. Training programmes are congested and opportunities to revise infantry tactics appear minimal.[20]

The most significant dictate of the (RM)CoS, is the continual movement of specialists on completion of every draft. As individuals leave on routine postings, moving back to their specialisations or professional courses, they are replaced by new personnel. This rotation means that training has to be constantly repeated, resulting in limited progression from the skeletal level achieved in basic training. In this tempo and with the continual replacement of personnel, there is a reliance on the Commando course being a sufficient guarantee. The assumption is that individuals, having passed Commando training, must therefore have a sufficient understanding of close-combat fighting and tactics. This assumption is tenuous and dangerously wrong; it takes years of study and practice to become proficient in infantry fighting. The following example illustrates the difficult training balance the approach creates.

In parts, Royal Marines close-combat teams train to exceptional levels

High-end infantry skills are central to collective tactical success. The Royal Marines' sniper course is considered the best of its type and tests the exact infantry skills which are the basis of close-combat performance. In 2015, due to a requirement for additional sniper team controllers, the course was undertaken by a chosen group of specialist Corporals. In spite of being specially selected, every one of these tactical commanders failed.[21] This result appears alarming but is not a reflection of their individual potential, these ranks were amongst the most talented personnel in the armed forces. The failure rate is an inevitable by-product of a workforce model that attempts to balance specialist trades with the training and conduct of close combat.

In parts, Royal Marines close-combat teams train to exceptional levels. The tasks they conduct are highly specialised and are almost unrecognisable from the traditional infantry role. These include counter-piracy, counter-narcotics or Joint Personnel Recovery; all are predominantly based on close quarter battle (CQB) drills. The Combat Boarding Operator SSQ is a pronounced example. Stuart Lyle, from the UK Defence Science and Technology Laboratory, recently commented: 'The Royal Marines are the best CQB specialists in conventional forces'.[22] Regardless of the level of capability these teams attain, the time spent in the positions is always limited to a single, brief cycle. It is mandatory to rotate out of this DCC role and train in a supporting specialisation, never allowing an individual to develop over time. In contrast, members of the new Ranger Regiment will be largely taken from dedicated infantry positions, undergo an arduous selection process then train to the highest infantry standard, often with US counterparts. Pivotally, they are then retained in that role.

Functions of Combat

In the liminal period of FCF design, there has been innovative change in Royal Marines force structure. ISTAR and fire support have been shaped to ensure the 'Find, Fix, Strike' functions of combat are achieved in the most effective ways. There has been substantial investment in reconnaissance, snipers, mortar and anti-tank teams, which are vital components in all tactical actions and a significant advance in the development of FCF lethality. Combat support is similar in character and naturally aligns to the DCC role. These specialisations require a range of skills but are distinctly different to close combat. A mortar fire controller learning to adjust intimate mortar support, or a sniper team calculating high-angle precision fire, differ from tactics used in the infantry assault. In an attempt to conduct several roles, the skill level drops in them all and atrophy is guaranteed.

Violence

In an era of constant warfighting, sections and platoons of UK battlegroups have been involved in hundreds of operations and thousands of small-arms contacts. These campaigns were the catalyst for

20. Author interview with 42 Commando RM, unit training officer, responsible for the conduct of DCC preparation and readiness, 2018.
21. Author interview with the Royal Marines sniper training team, responsible for the delivery of this course, 2015, and follow-up conversations.
22. @Stuart_Lyle, 'Cracking footage and shows just why the Royal Marines are the best CQB specialists in the conventional forces. Having observed their advanced CQB course & other training, I can confirm it is intense. Essential for their specialist roles. *Caveat* - CQB alone is not #urbanwarfare' [Twitter post], 10:12am, 8 October 2022 <https://twitter.com/stu_lyle/status/1578674658563411969?s=46&t=97AGiTK4663C429RyyLtA>, accessed 17 March 2023.

British forces to re-learn the art of tactical fighting. The violence of these battles pressure tested marksmanship and tactics, refining infantry skill and building deep, tactical knowledge. Operations proved to be an acid test of battle drills, eliminating anything that did not work, anything that was superfluous in contact. Because of the confused and extremely difficult nature of counterinsurgency, battles sometimes continued for weeks and months throughout deployments and tactical success was difficult to achieve: contacts were often 'protracted and indecisive'.[23] In this ferocious kinetic fighting, close-combat soldiers eventually learnt how to achieve success in tactical fighting.

It is essential to retain this experience so the granular lessons that were learnt can be re-taught, and UK combat forces are prepared for future conflicts. The (RM)CoS design means all the close-combat personnel who conducted this fighting, are rotated back into their respective specialisations. The constant rotation from supporting roles, through to close combat, and returning to a support role is a difficult balance; one which creates an enduring tactical dilemma. This rich seam of learning is continuously diluted. Experience is generally retained within the wider Royal Marines framework but dispersed, it evaporates from the front-line units responsible for close-combat fighting. Having learnt from months of violence, individuals are then moved into positions where that experience is immediately redundant, and which then stays largely irrelevant.

Operational Case Study

In discussion with experienced, senior non-commissioned officers, one six-month operational tour was cited as a typical example of how this (RM) CoS system works in practice.

Operation *Herrick 9* in Afghanistan, which took place from 2008 to 2009, was famous for its complexity and level of violence. It is used here to illustrate the difficulty of retaining experience due to the (RM)CoS model.

On recovery to the UK, a specialist landing-craftsman, who acted as a section-level commander throughout this operation, returned to HMS *Ocean*, spending the majority of his career as a coxswain of the larger utility craft. Two machine-gunners were ordered to train as drivers and used from that point on in the motor-transport department. As a measure of their potential, both immediately applied for, then successfully passed training for UK Special Forces; one joining the Defence Human-intelligence Unit, the second transitioning to the Special Reconnaissance Regiment. In the Royal Marines, even with their volume of tactical experience, having learnt so much from the previous six months of warfighting, both were employed as civilian coach drivers on a naval base in Scotland. Within an 18-month period after the operational tour had ended, every single rank who had been involved in the fighting had moved out of the platoon studied. Most had trained in a Royal Marines specialisation, others had returned to their dedicated support roles or changed service. The fighting experience had entirely gone from the platoon, dissipated around Royal Marines specialisations and broader Defence. In a comparable army infantry company, there would be little movement of personnel; this knowledge, earnt through vicious fighting and now indispensable, would largely be retained. These examples are not anomalies or exceptions; this is the normal, routine process. Individuals are directed to train in supporting roles, irrespective of ability or experience. Notably, commanders at every level, routinely move back into their respective specialisations.

Atavism

A Declinist Approach

'The Royal Marines have been long regarded as one of the best and most proficient regiments in NATO'.[24] Indeed, the Royal Marines has a culture of physical excellence, a culture which nurtures outstanding moral and behavioural standards. Throughout every unit of the Royal Marines, there is a tangible atmosphere of pride, and the iconic Green Beret has become a symbol of excellence and achievement. Deleteriously, the way in which the Royal Marines is organised causes a tactical paradox. There is an intrinsic error in the physical component that significantly affects the conceptual. Specifically, from the point of tactical performance, the (RM) CoS is a fragmentary approach; it inhibits consistent study and practise of the close-combat role. Against foundational text and the prescriptive orthodoxy of the regimental system, the (RM)CoS approach interrupts and congests the close-combat function. This system is unique to the Royal Marines, who, isolated from the mass of infantry regiments, are

23. Jim Storr, 'Manoeuvre and Weapons Effect on the Battlefield', *RUSI Defence Systems*, 2010, p. 61.
24. King, *The Combat Soldier, Infantry Tactics and Cohesion in the Twentieth and Twenty-First Centuries*, p. 319.

unaware of their own fragility. Using the core tactical skills of Live Firing Marksmanship Training (LFMT) and LFTT to measure ability, in direct competition the army infantry achieves markedly higher levels of performance. Perceived advantages in physical and education standards become irrelevant, as the infantry is able to progressively learn over time. Specificity and high performance are indivisible, as these objective tests prove. It may be an unpalatable truth to Royal Marines, who are considered the elite, but it is the army who prove tactically more adept.

In an era of ostentatious divisional support, in which air superiority and ISTAR assets immediately overmatched the enemy, Royal Marines units had time to revise and adjust to the DCC role. Their performance on recent operations is a testament of their intelligence and agility. Against a highly motivated, capable peer army, the FCF will not have this luxury. Lacking mass and scaled with limited fire support,[25] skill in close combat becomes imperative.

A Revanchist Design for Close Combat

In his 1939 book, *The Defence of Britain*, the famous strategist BH Liddell Hart states: 'A landing on a foreign coast in the face of hostile troops has always been one of the most difficult operations of war'.[26] Due to the proliferation of modern A2/AD systems, this has now become an extremely dangerous offensive action. Royal Marines planners envisage small, highly versatile FCF teams, attacking key enemy targets. This concept of disaggregated infiltration tactics means it is essential every Marine in a close-combat role is trained to an excellent level. Any degree of critical thinking applied to the current Royal Marines workforce model will recognise that it is a poor means to achieve this expectation. Against a backdrop of state-on-state land war in Europe, Royal Marines command should again recognise the importance of its core infantry nature. The appointment of a new commandant general in December 2022 is an opportunity to direct change, re-thinking the (RM)CoS approach to close combat.

A combination of understanding, structural change and a revanchist attitude to tactical excellence, will concentrate focus on close combat; the 'raison-d'etre' of the Royal Marines. This will make FCF teams dramatically more effective and more lethal. In 'Insights for Contemporary Amphibious Operations', General Julian Thompson states: 'It is much better to start with a basic Infantry unit which you then train to split off'.[27] Flexibility is then generated not by rotating CSS ranks through the infantry role, but through training these supporting ranks to conduct broader activities. Additional reliance on Royal Navy services or army units is unnecessary, and the current force model is simply streamed into fixed roles, which ensures specificity.

The ideal FCF model would include a dedicated infantry component. DCC would be considered a PSQ, with a restriction of one SSQ. This retains specificity and ensures personnel within FCF Strike companies are proficient in close combat and its enabling skills such as assault-breacher or combat-marksman. Resources such as personal equipment and ammunition can then be massed at the point of lethality, reinforcing the DCC function and allowing teams to achieve an advanced level of marksmanship and tactical proficiency. Deep conceptual study intertwined with specific, consistent training will develop agile, adept teams, highly creative in the pursuit of tactical success.

This reform will trigger cascades of discussion, the coordinating details are significant and the decision to transmute decisive. But, however difficult the organisational change, as the character of FCF battlegroup capability is being shaped, DCC lethality must have absolute priority.

This immediately changes FCF teams into a truly elite combat force. The Royal Marines can then deliver a message with substance: that the FCF now has the highest calibre of close-combat troops. Given the excellent potential of the Royal Marines, this is an achievable and realistic aspiration. ■

James White recently left the military after 22 years of service. He was a Royal Marines Sniper with operational experience in Sierra Leone, Northern Ireland, Iraq and Afghanistan. During his time in the Royal Marines, he was Close Combat Tactical Commander, Sniper Team Commander; Senior Instructor – Army Infantry Battle School, Brecon and units throughout the Royal Marines; responsible for the tuition and conduct of tactics and marksmanship.

25. See Jack Watling, 'The Future of Fires, Maximising the UK's Tactical and Operational Firepower', *RUSI Occasional Papers* (November 2019), p. 2. The UK's most deployable formations – 16 Air Assault Brigade and 3 Command Brigade – can each field two batteries of six 105-mm L118 light guns as their entire fires capability.
26. BH Liddell Hart, *The Defence of Britain* (New York, NY: Random House, 1939), p. 130.
27. Julian Thompson, 'Falklands 40: Insights for Contemporary Amphibious Operations', RUSI online event, 5 July 2022.

Research Article
RUSI Journal

South Korea's Expanding Arms Trade with the Middle East

From Workers to Weapons

Shirzad Azad

The Republic of Korea (South Korea) has emerged surprisingly to secure some lucrative defence export deals with several countries across the Middle East in recent years. In this article, Shirzad Azad tries to shed some light on how the Korean defence industry is extensively courting the bustling arms markets in the Middle East to advance its ongoing ambitious military programmes at home, and achieve greater financial gains from its enhanced industrial capabilities and scientific knowhow in this critical field.

South Korea's engagement with the greater Middle East region, including North Africa, has developed at astonishing speed; over the course of less than half a century, it has moved from exporting human labour to supplying high-grade military products. The East Asian country's export forays into the region began in the aftermath of the first oil shock of 1973, when it dispatched large numbers of unskilled workers and inexperienced contractors to work primarily for the Western and Japanese construction companies active in the Middle East. By the mid-1980s, more than one million unskilled labourers and hundreds of construction companies from South Korea benefitted from the petrodollars flowing into major oil-exporting countries across the Middle East, enabling it to finance a great deal of its fledgling industrialisation and economic development programmes.[1] Apart from exporting workers to the Middle East in the wake of the first and second oil shocks, South Korea gradually tapped into every other profitable and promising market in the region, including arms deals.[2]

Although South Korea played a cameo role in the Middle Eastern arms markets in the early 1980s, its involvement was simultaneously insignificant and surreptitious. South Korea still needed several decades before it could emerge as a relatively credible merchant to promote its military innovations among Middle Eastern countries. The long interval had much to do with South Korea's own struggle to modernise its defence industry and devise various new and coveted military equipment sufficiently high-tech to enter the competitive arms markets of the Middle East. At the same time, the flow of non-arms Korean products to the region never dwindled through the decades, as major South Korean brands of automobiles and electronic devices captured a significant share of consumption in many Middle Eastern countries. By the time South Korea had produced a number of world-class military products, it already had a good reputation and enough experience in non-military fields to know where and how to find markets for its arms and defence technologies in the region.[3]

In examining South Korea's major arms deals with several Middle Eastern nations in recent years,

1. U Shim, 'Korea's Economic Progress Owes Much to Saudi Arabia', *Diplomacy* (Vol. 9, No. 11, 1983), pp. 30–31.
2. John Lie, *Han Unbound: The Political Economy of South Korea* (Stanford, CA: Stanford University Press, 1998), pp. 87–88.
3. Richard A Bitzinger, *Towards a Brave New Arms Industry?* (Oxford: Oxford University Press, 2003), Adelphi Papers, Vol. 43, No. 356, p. 52.

Prototype of the KF-21 Boramae, April 2021. *Courtesy of Newscom / BJ Warnick / Alamy*

this article argues that the country is getting a head start on the region as very fertile ground to advance its burgeoning defence industry. As the Middle East has been in the crosshairs of almost all prominent Western and Eastern producers of armaments over the past several decades, it seems natural for successive conservative and liberal governments in South Korea to earmark the region as a potentially big customer for its arms products. This research is also based on the hypothesis that South Korea has long been cognisant of its limits and boundaries in the Middle East's bustling arms markets, despite demonstrating a great enthusiasm to sign a number of lucrative defence contracts with countries in the region. In particular, as Korean defence industry and military innovations have largely been a state-sponsored endeavour, international alliance politics has not allowed the East Asian country to sell its defence products to Iran, despite the omnipresence of non-military South Korean goods throughout Iranian markets during the past two decades.

This raises the issue of external constraints, especially the US factor, in South Korea's aspiration to cement its position as one of the world's leading arms manufacturers and a key supplier of arms products. Unlike the 1970s, when Washington was quite willing to impose certain sanctions on South Korea to force Seoul into giving up its quest for acquiring nuclear weapons, it seems that the US has made its peace with the Korean ambition to become a leading supplier of conventional arms and munitions in the world as long as South Korea keeps selling its defence products to the countries which are perceived to be friendly, or at least neutral, toward the US and the West in general.[4] In recent years, South Korea has generally followed this yardstick in terms of signing major arms deals with several nations in the Middle East and other regions. There is also the possibility that the US is 'rewarding' South Korea by letting it emerge as a leading player in the global armaments market in exchange for increasing cooperation between Washington and Seoul regarding a whole host of hot-

4. *New York Times*, 'Seoul Officials Say Strong Pressure Forced Cancellation of Plans to Purchase a French Nuclear Plant', 1 February 1976, p. 11. See also Daniel W Drezner, *The Sanctions Paradox: Economic Statecraft and International Relations* (Cambridge: Cambridge University Press, 1999), p. 255.

DOI: 10.1080/03071847.2023.2218892

button regional and international matters, including the Iranian nuclear issue.[5]

Figure 1: Regional Share of the World's Total Arms Imports, 2017–20

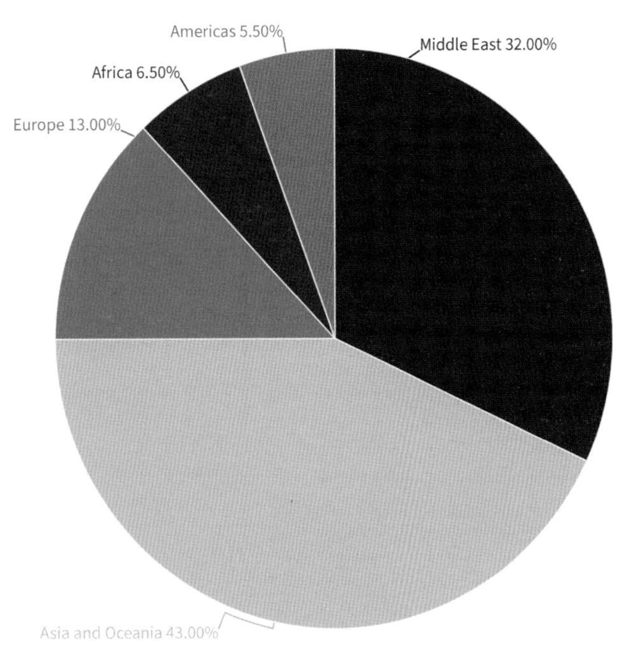

Source: SIPRI, *SIPRI Yearbook 2021* (Oxford University Press, 2021).

Framework of Analysis: Evolving as a Self-Assertive Arms Exporter

Since its formal establishment in August 1948, South Korea emerged as a security state which had to pay enormous attention to military power to survive. The Korean War between 1950–53, and the ongoing antagonistic relationship between Seoul and Pyongyang, only re-enforced the paramount importance of security and defence calculations in almost every aspect of domestic and foreign policymaking in South Korea.[6] More importantly, in the early 1960s when South Korea embarked in earnest upon a national agenda of industrialisation and economic development, its ensuing strategy of mercantile realism identified technological progress and wealth creation as being as critical as military strength to succeed and thrive. As expected and sanctioned by the conventional realist theory of international relations, South Korea's economic growth and technological accomplishments were to translate directly into additional military power and defence capabilities. It all paved the way for the Korean military industrial complex to advance in lockstep with the country's economic and technological progress.[7]

The South Korean government, therefore, turned out to play a vital role by investing lavish military and defence spending one decade after another. Indeed, for a whole host of reasons, including fierce rivalry with North Korea as well as South Korea's own military modernisation plans, successive governments in Seoul needed to pay special attention to military capabilities. The private sector, including some South Korean conglomerates (*chaebol*), were also provided with assistance and perks to invest early in certain military technologies and defence products.[8] Another equally critical factor was the role of foreign technology and military support, a bulk of which was underwritten by the US. For several decades from the late 1940s onward, South Korea was among the main recipients of US weapons and military aid, relying on Washington for almost all of the advanced arms and munitions it needed to import.[9] In addition, South Korea sent tens of thousands of its officers and military technicians to

5. Shirzad Azad, 'Perks and Perils of Strategic Choice: South Korea's Iran Policy under Moon Jae-in', *East Asia* (Vol. 39, No. 4, 2022), pp. 371–87; Cho Chung-un, 'US Exempts Korea from Export Restrictions on Russia', *Korea Herald*, 8 March 2022, <https://www.koreaherald.com/common/newsprint.php?ud=20220308000597>, accessed 11 December 2022; and Joel Atkinson, '"K-Defense" Arms Exports Are Tying South Korea to the United States', *The National Interest*, 7 September 2022, <https://nationalinterest.org/blog/korea-watch/'k-defense'-arms-exports-are-tying-south-korea-united-states-204636>, accessed 17 February 2023.
6. US Congress, Office of Technology Assessment, *Global Arms Trade*, OTA-ISC-460 (Washington, DC: US Government Printing Office, June 1991), p. 131.
7. Ralph Pettman, *Commonsense Constructivism, or the Making of World Affairs* (London and New York, NY: Routledge, 2000), p. 168.
8. The term *chaebol* refers to a large family-owned and family-run business conglomerate. It combines the two words of *chae* (wealth) and *bol* (clan) in the Korean language. For more information regarding the relationship between the *Chaebol* and government in South Korea, see Yeon-ho Lee, *The State, Society and Big Business in South Korea* (London and New York, NY: Routledge, 1997).
9. Nicholas L Miller, *Stopping the Bomb: The Sources and Effectiveness of US Nonproliferation Policy* (Ithaca, NY and London: Cornell University Press, 2018), p. 138.

the US, who became instrumental in transferring the relevant American defence knowledge to South Korea.[10] Aside from enjoying such benefits, South Korea had been allowed to produce some types of weapons under licence, or even develop them based on their original US technology.[11]

As a result, South Korea is now one of the largest exporters of arms and defence products in the world, although it has also remained one of the world's biggest arms importers.[12] Of the world's top 100 defence contractors, four companies are South Korean, including Hanwha, Korea Aerospace Industries, LIG Nex1 and Hyundai Rotem. According to *SIPRI Yearbook 2021*, South Korea was the ninth largest arms supplier between 2016–2020, accounting for 2.7% of total military exports worldwide. Data updated by *SIPRI Yearbook 2022* shows that South Korea could supply 2.8% of the world's total export of arms and munitions between 2017 and 2021, positioning itself as the eighth biggest exporter of armaments during that period. This is a significant boost compared with its 0.9% share of the world's total arms exports in the period 2011–2015.[13] In 2021 alone, South Korea could export arms and defence products worth roughly $7 billion, and that figure increased at a phenomenal rate, to about $17 billion in 2022 – partly because of South Korea's high-value arms deals with a number of Middle Eastern countries.[14] Such figures signify a remarkable improvement in South Korea's arms exports compared with two decades earlier when all the military products which the South Koreans were selling to other countries earned little more than $200 million.[15]

The South Korean government turned out to play a vital role by investing lavish military and defence spending one decade after another

South Korea's turbocharged military progress and defence products have, therefore, made it very ambitious in its unflinching quest for capturing a larger share of the world's arms markets. And, regardless of which political party pulls the strings in Seoul, there is almost no difference across the political spectrum with regard to upgrading the country's military innovations and selling its products to other nations.[16] In recent years, the South Koreans have been striving to promote their arms and defence products across the world; from Oceania to Latin America and from Asia to Africa.[17] Aside from winning over several loyal and long-term customers, they have engaged in serious negotiations and arms deals with a number of industrialised and developed Western countries. After South Korea signed a major arms deal, valued at more than $700 million in December 2021, to supply Australia with an artillery system developed by Hanwha, for example, Hyundai Rotem increased its marketing and promotional efforts among some

10. Andrew J Pierre, *The Global Politics of Arms Sales* (Princeton, NJ: Princeton University Press, 1982), pp. 210–11.
11. SIPRI (Stockholm International Peace Research Institute), *SIPRI Yearbook 2011: Armaments, Disarmament and International Security* (New York, NY: Oxford University Press, 2011), p. 241.
12. In the period between 2017 and 2021, South Korea was the seventh biggest importer of armaments, bringing in more than 4% of the world's total arms products. SIPRI, *SIPRI Yearbook 2022: Armaments, Disarmament and International Security, Summary* (Oxford University Press, 2022), p. 13.
13. SIPRI, *SIPRI Yearbook 2021* (Oxford University Press; 2021), p. 15; and *SIPRI Yearbook 2022*, p. 13.
14. Kyung-Min Kang, Jeong Min Nam and Young Chan Song, 'S.Korea's Defense Exports to Top $10 Billion', *Korea Economic Daily*, 17 January 2022, <https://www.kedglobal.com/newsView/ked202201170016>, accessed 17 March 2022; and *Yonhap News Agency*, 'S. Korea Ranks 8th in World Arms Exports: Report', 9 December 2022, <https://en.yna.co.kr/view/AEN20221209005700325>, accessed 17 February 2023.
15. Bitzinger, *Towards a Brave New Arms Industry?*, p. 52.
16. For instance, South Korea's proposed defence budget for 2023 is around 57.1 trillion won ($42.3 billion), of which more than 10% will be allocated for advancing 'a number of development and acquisition projects, including the third mass-production run of K2 Black Panther battle tanks, the construction of FFX Batch III guided-missile frigates, and the procurement of reserve combat ammunition'. Gabriel Dominguez, 'Seoul Proposes 4.6% Hike in Defense Spending for 2023', *Japan Times*, 31 August 2022, <https://www.japantimes.co.jp/news/2022/08/31/asia-pacific/seoul-hike-defense-spending-2023/>, accessed 19 February 2023.
17. Kim Jaewon, 'South Korean Arms Makers in Spotlight after Missile Limit Lifted', *Nikkei Asia*, 2 June 2021, <https://asia.nikkei.com/Business/Aerospace-Defense/South-Korean-arms-makers-in-spotlight-after-missile-limit-lifted>, accessed 27 October 2022.

north European countries, Norway in particular, to sell its next-generation battle tanks.[18]

South Korea has pushed for almost any type of defence deal with as many Middle Eastern countries as its international alliance politics will allow it to enter into arms agreements with

In comparison with other geographical regions, however, the Middle East has attracted the South Korean defence industry in terms of materialising the most expensive arms deals in its history. In 2021 alone, the greater Middle East region, including North Africa, spent approximately $205.6 billion on armaments, accounting for 9.7% of the world's total military expenditure.[19] With similarities to offering the largest construction deals to Korean contractors in the post-oil shocks building bonanza, the region is now regarded as a major engine of growth for the Korean defence industry, galvanising the Korean government and its Middle East-based diplomatic missions into action. Many energy and cash-rich nations across the Middle East have long been a target market for the world's prominent arms producers, and South Korea has just recently begun to seriously compete with its more experienced Western and Eastern rivals, signing dozens of high-value arms contracts in the region.[20] From selling tear gas to Bahrain, to exporting more expensive military products to some other Arab sheikhdoms in the region, South Korea has pushed for almost any type of defence deal with as many Middle Eastern countries as its international alliance politics will allow it to enter into arms agreements with. Although the history of South Korea's arms agreements with the Middle East is several decades old, in recent years a number of up-and-coming countries in the region provided better business opportunities for the Korean military industrial complex.

Table 1: The World's Top 10 Exporters of Armaments, 2017–21

Country	Percentage share
United States	39
Russia	19
France	11
China	4.6
Germany	4.5
Italy	3.1
Britain	2.9
South Korea	2.8
Spain	2.5
Israel	2.4

Source: SIPRI, *SIPRI Yearbook 2021* (Oxford University Press, 2021).

The Iran–Iraq War: The First Experience that Whetted the Appetite

As a major long-lasting and devastating military conflict in the 20th century, the Iran–Iraq War turned the entire Middle East virtually into a top bazaar of armaments, enticing almost every arms producer in the West and the East to join the race to enter the region's profitable markets of defence products. In addition to the two superpowers of the time, the US and the Soviet Union, most great powers and a slew of smaller ones all strived to sell their armaments of various types to Iran and Iraq.[21] South Korea was among those small yet ambitious states that wished to take advantage of its officially declared diplomatic position (neutrality) toward the two warring Middle Eastern countries and sell to both of them. By the time the Iran–Iraq War started, South Korea's arms exports to the outside world were all but nonexistent, and the swiftly-developing and industrialising nation was something of an unknown quantity in the international arms markets. Yet this did not deter it.[22]

While South Korea could technically ship as many weapons to Iraq as desired, its potential

18. Colin Packham, 'Australia Signs $717 Million Defence Deal with South Korea's Hanwha', *Reuters*, 13 December 2021.
19. SIPRI, 'SIPRI Fact Sheet: Trends in World Military Expenditure, 2021', April 2022, <https://www.sipri.org/sites/default/files/2022-04/fs_2204_milex_2021_0.pdf>, accessed 29 April 2023.
20. Pierre, *The Global Politics of Arms Sales*, pp. 155–56.
21. Adam Tarock, *The Superpowers' Involvement in the Iran–Iraq War* (Commack, NY: Nova Science Publishers, 1998), p. 49.
22. Michael Brzoska, 'Profiteering on the Iran–Iraq War', *Bulletin of the Atomic Scientists* (Vol. 43, No. 5, June 1987), pp. 42–45.

arms deals with Iran had already encountered serious impediments. The US had regulated South Korea's arms exports, and any substantial transfer of sensitive dual-use technologies by the Koreans was under severe restrictions. South Korea also could not engage in significant arms deals with the countries which Washington had blackballed as state sponsors of terrorism or designated as violators of human rights.[23] In addition, Iran had come under international arms embargoes in the wake of its ongoing hostile relationship with Western countries, the US in particular, making it very difficult for major arms producers to supply arms to Tehran overtly; that was one of the reasons why China had to use North Korea as a conduit to sell weapons to Iran in the early period of the Iran–Iraq War, before Beijing decided to do away with the intermediary role of Pyongyang and directly engage in arms transactions with Tehran.[24]

South Korea was also pressed by a number of Middle Eastern countries, especially Saudi Arabia, not to supply arms to Iran at the cost of Iraq, which was then receiving political, financial, and even military support provided by many nations in the region and beyond.[25] That was probably a reason why South Korea encountered few problems, if any, when engaging in several important arms agreements with the Ba'ath regime of Iraq, led by Saddam Hussein. The US, moreover, could look the other way when South Korea's arms business with Baghdad was sharply contradicting a number of its military restrictions and regulatory controls over South Korea's weapons exports, including the sale of armaments to nations involved in regional conflicts. After all, many in South Korea were then arguing that their arms deals with Saddam were actually in sync with the US policy to isolate Iran further and weaken its military power.[26]

The statistics published about the entire South Korean weapons exports during the Iran–Iraq War revealed South Korea's somewhat complicated and possibly murky arms connections with the two warring parties in the Middle East. At the outset of the Middle East conflict, South Korea's export of military equipment was less than $200 million. But in 1982, the Korean arms exports suddenly rose to $975 million; a figure which signified a five-fold jump in its earnings from selling weapons to other countries, Iran and Iraq in particular. Its military products and arms exports to the region consisted largely of some conventional weapons and low-tech equipment such as tanks, patrol boats, small arms, and uniforms. In the following year, its income from arms exports plummeted to around $370 million, though it was still a significant achievement for a second-tier arms merchant at that time.[27] In 1988 when the Iran–Iraq War concluded, South Korea could earn only $50 million for its sale of weapons and munitions to the outside world.[28]

Meanwhile, there were some reports concerning the potential involvement of South Korea in the Iran–Contra scandal, which took place during the final years of the Iran–Iraq war and coincided with the second term of the Reagan presidency in the US. It was essentially a covert operation of arms sales to Iran to fund the Contra rebels who were then fighting the leftist government of Nicaragua.[29] When the incident fizzled out, South Korea became part of a US congressional investigation to find out whether it had supplied US weapons to Iran by playing a middleman role for the US, similar to what North Korea had already done on behalf of China.[30] Moreover, Donald Gregg, who was a key figure behind the Iran–Contra affair, was appointed as the US ambassador to South Korea from 1989 to 1993. At the time of the scandal, Gregg was serving as Vice President George Bush's National Security Advisor. Despite public disbelief and a great deal of media scrutiny in the US, both Gregg and South

23. Eiichi Katahara, 'Japan's Concept of Comprehensive Security in the Post-Cold War World', in Susan L Shirk and Christopher P Twomey (eds.), *Power and Prosperity: Economics and Security Linkages in Asia–Pacific* (New Brunswick, NJ: Transaction Publishers, 1996), pp. 213–32.
24. Guy Burton, *China and Middle East Conflicts: Responding to War and Rivalry from the Cold War to the Present* (Abingdon and New York, NY: Routledge, 2020), p. 80.
25. William D Hartung, 'US–Korea Jet Deal Boosts Arms Trade', *Bulletin of the Atomic Scientists* (Vol. 46, No. 9, 1990), pp. 18–24.
26. Janne E Nolan, *Military Industry in Taiwan and South Korea* (London and New York, NY: Palgrave Macmillan, 1986), p. 175.
27. David J Louscher and Michael D Salomone, *Technology Transfer and U.S. Security Assistance: The Impact of Licensed Production* (Boulder, CO: Westview Press, 1987), p. 161.
28. Williamson Murray and Kevin M Woods, *The Iran–Iraq War: A Military and Strategic History* (Cambridge: Cambridge University Press, 2014), p. 316.
29. Robert Busby, *Reagan and the Iran–Contra Affair: The Politics of Presidential Recovery* (New York, NY: St. Martin's Press, 1999), p. 55.
30. Shirzad Azad, 'Evolving Toward Normalcy amid Anomaly: North Korea's Middle East Policy since the Demise of Kim Il-Sung', *Asian Affairs* (Vol. 49, No. 3, 2018), pp. 383–401.

Korea emerged unscathed from the relevant criminal investigations.[31]

The First, Largest Export: Arms Deals with Post-Saddam Iraq

For all its trial-and-error arms connections with the Middle East during the Iran–Iraq War in the 1980s, South Korea kept a close eye on the region as a promising market for its aspiring defence industry.[32] As an incubator of regional conflicts and a hotbed of interstate rivalry, the Middle East was always likely to remain a prime destination for the world's major military products, much the same as it had carried on its security affairs and arms transactions prior to the outbreak of the Iran–Iraq War. Despite paying careful attention to certain Western diktats concerning arms deals with some Middle Eastern countries in the post-Cold War era, the South Koreans were prepared to export occasionally and surreptitiously some of their armaments and defence items to the region, supported by their experiences from the 1980s. Between 2000 and 2002, for instance, the pariah Iraqi state under Saddam Hussein brought in thousands of supply and transport vehicles for its elite Republican Guard, and South Korea happened to be one of the primary suppliers of those vehicles.[33]

Still, better days for South Korea and its military industrial complex in Iraq had to wait until the US removed Saddam Hussein in 2003. The Iraq War and its aftermath were a rare international occasion for South Korea to demonstrate its close cooperation with Washington, as the liberal government of Roh Moo-hyun dispatched some 3,600 soldiers and army medics to Iraq to provide various logistical support for US-led troops amid fierce domestic opposition with regard to Seoul's policy behaviour. The Korean troops sent to Iraq formed the third largest contingent of foreign forces after the US and British military combatants.[34] As a consequence, South Korea took advantage of the war to break the taboo of sending its soldiers to a perilous and unpredictable war zone far away from the Korean Peninsula, although its forces were largely stationed in relatively safer parts of northern Iraq. South Korea would later build on this critical experience by dispatching its marines to nearby waters on patrol missions, using such practices to showcase its enhanced military power and defence capabilities.[35]

The Korean approach toward the war provided opportunities for a closer long-term partnership between South Korea and the post-Saddam political system of Iraq. For decades, South Korea had been struggling to enter the untapped construction market of Iraq, but incessant military conflicts and international sanctions had made it impossible for Korean contractors to benefit sufficiently from the Middle Eastern country. Besides offering a prospective building market after the war, Iraq was to emerge as a major crude producer in the region after the flow of foreign investments and technologies, partly by Korean companies, into its dilapidated oil industry. Once larger cargoes of crude were exported, and higher oil revenues filled the Iraqi state's coffers, politicians in Baghdad carved out a host of plans to reconstruct various shattered areas of their war-torn country. Engulfed by myriad security challenges internally and externally, Iraq soon focused on refurbishing its military and defence capabilities by entering into several significant weapons procurements involving other countries, including South Korea.[36]

In December 2013, the Iraqi government signed a staggering $1.1 billion agreement to buy 24 T-50 light fighter jets from South Korea. In the following year, the two sides agreed another $1 billion deal permitting South Korea to provide parts, equipment and pilot training for those aircraft. Clinching the most expensive arms shipment in the history of South Korean weapons exports, Korea Aerospace Industries (KAI) was obliged by the lucrative deal, valued at more than $2 billion in total, to deliver to Iraq the T-50IQ aircrafts, a variant of the Korean T-50 supersonic fighter jets, by 2017.[37] Apart from huge financial gain for South Korea, the unprecedented

---

31. James McEnteer, *Deep in the Heart: The Texas Tendency in American Politics* (Westport, CT: Praeger, 2004), p. 270.
32. Ian Bowers, *The Modernisation of the Republic of Korea Navy: Seapower, Strategy and Politics* (New York, NY: Palgrave Macmillan, 2018), p. 177.
33. John F Murphy, *The Evolving Dimensions of International Law: Hard Choices for the World Community* (New York, NY: Cambridge University Press, 2010), p. 131.
34. Thomas Hubbard, 'Chapter 9: USA Ambassador to ROK 2001–2004', *Ambassadors' Memoir: U.S.–Korea Relations through the Eyes of the Ambassadors* (Washington, DC: The Korea Economic Institute, 2009), p. 186.
35. Bowers, *The Modernisation of the Republic of Korea Navy*, p. 177.
36. Daniel Serwer, 'Muddling Through in Iraq', *Survival* (Vol. 55, No. 4, 2013), pp. 35–40.
37. In 2005 the T-50 Golden Eagle supersonic trainer entered active service in South Korea after KAI and the US defence company Lockheed Martin had co-developed the light fighter jet. In 2022, South Korea's export of armaments racked up

arms agreement was also an important diplomatic victory for the South Korean government because Iraq had already ordered 36 F-16 fighter jets from the US but the Americans had continually refused to deliver them to Baghdad citing various security, political, and human rights concerns.[38]

In fact, Iraq was determined to rebuild its air force as well as other branches of the Iraqi armed forces at an extremely trying time when Baghdad had to fight the spreading tentacles of the mysterious Islamic State. To achieve their ambitious defence objective quickly, the new Iraqi leaders were willing to go out of their way by negotiating a number of weapons pacts with non-Western nations, including South Korea.[39] As an outcome of Baghdad's sustainable arms agreements with Seoul after the lucrative 2013 deal, Iraq could position itself as the second biggest market, after Turkey, for South Korean arms exports in 2016 and 2017. In 2018 Korea's top three customers of arms and munitions were Indonesia, Iraq and Britain.[40] When South Korea unexpectedly emerged as the 10th biggest exporter of weapons and defence products in the world the following year, Iraq was still the second largest client of Korean armaments after Indonesia, and subsequently raised the possibility of giving a more contentious arms order to Korea.[41]

The order relates to acquiring a highly advanced air defence system that could cover the entire sovereign territory of the Iraqi state. Negotiations are still underway as to whether Iraq can eventually purchase a sophisticated air defence system from France, South Korea or Russia. The US has adamantly opposed the idea of Iraq buying an S-400 air defence system from Russia, as Washington regards this move as contrary to its vested strategic interests in the wider Middle East region. The US does not want to lose its current aerial hegemony in the region, nor does it wish a Russian air defence system to be put in place that could displace the current defence superiority of their close Middle Eastern allies, especially Israel.[42] Under such a grinding stalemate, the US may ultimately compromise by letting the Iraqi government purchase a South Korean air defence system to avoid furthering a relationship between the Middle East and Russia, with the associated substantial security and political repercussions.

Growing Military and Arms Partnership with Turkey

The nature and scope of South Korea's relationship with Turkey differ from its ties with many other Middle Eastern countries. South Korea and Turkey cemented their deep and long-term connections several years before they commenced their official diplomatic relations. Following the onset of the Korean War, Turkey sent some 15,000 of its soldiers, making Ankara the fourth biggest supplier of foreign troops among the 16 countries which entered the war in favour of South Korea. Turkey was the only Middle Eastern nation that got involved in the Korean War, and more than 720 Turkish soldiers died in addition to many more Turkish forces who were maimed and wounded over the course of the internecine conflict.[43] Turkey gained some immediate benefits from its active participation in the war, including membership to the North Atlantic Treaty Organization (NATO) in 1952, but the development played a crucial role in various aspects of Korean–Turkish ties, including their security and military cooperation, for the decades to come.[44]

---

a new record after it signed a number of lucrative arms deals with Poland worth several billions of dollars, making it the biggest experience of exporting defence products to another country in the history of the Korean strategic military industry. Sehun Cheon and Joonsoo Park, 'South Korea Becoming Top-tier Global Arms Merchant', *Asia Times*, 16 December 2022, <https://asiatimes.com/2022/12/south-korea-becoming-top-tier-global-arms-merchant/>, accessed 17 February 2023; and Yang Han, 'South Korea Increases Arms Sales to Record High', *China Daily*, 14 November 2022, <https://www.chinadaily.com.cn/a/202211/14/WS6371a35da310491754329808.html>, accessed 18 February 2023.

38. Kang Seung-woo and Joint Press Corps, 'Korea Exports 24 Attack Jets to Iraq', *Korea Times*, 12 December 2013, <https://www.koreatimes.co.kr/www/news/nation/2015/08/205_147894.html>, accessed 14 November 2021.
39. Shirzad Azad, 'Breathing New Life into an Old Approach: The Looking-East Policy of the Post-war Iraq', *Journal of Contemporary Iraq & the Arab World* (Vol. 16, No. 3, 2022), pp. 217–33.
40. SIPRI, 'SIPRI Fact Sheet: Trends in International Arms Transfers, 2018', March 2019, <https://www.sipri.org/sites/default/files/2019-03/fs_1903_at_2018.pdf>, accessed 7 May 2023.
41. Josh Smith, 'S. Korea Opens Largest Defence Expo amid N. Korea Missile Tests', *Reuters*, 19 October 2021.
42. Inder Singh Bisht, 'Iraq Seeking "Russian, French, or South Korean" Air Defense System', *Defense Post*, 12 October 2021, <https://www.thedefensepost.com/2021/10/12/iraq-foreign-air-defense-system/>, accessed 11 March 2022.
43. Steven Casey, *Selling the Korean War: Propaganda, Politics, and Public Opinion in the United States, 1950–1953* (New York, NY: Oxford University Press, 2008), pp. 29–30.
44. Soner Cagaptay, *The New Sultan: Erdogan and the Crisis of Modern Turkey* (London and New York, NY: IB Tauris, 2017), p. 51.

Like South Korea, Turkey was governed for some time by military rulers who demonstrated a great keenness for security and military affairs. More precisely, Turkey began to develop in earnest its arms industry in the 1970s, after its invasion of Cyprus in 1974 and the ensuing US arms embargo against Ankara. Interestingly, the US also imposed sanctions on South Korea in the 1970s for its clandestine attempts to acquire nuclear weapons. Another common feature of their developing defence industry was that Turkey remained a major importer of foreign arms and munitions before it was able to become an important exporter of armaments in the past decade.[45] As late as 1999, for instance, Turkey was the third biggest importer of arms and munitions in the world. It took the Turks another two decades before they could emerge as the world's 14th largest supplier of defence products in 2018 by exporting arms valued at around $2.2 billion; although the Middle Eastern country still had to bring in a great deal of its required advanced weaponry from other countries, including South Korea.[46]

Turkey's defence industry has, therefore, expanded exponentially over the past several years, paving the ground for a number of more successful Turkish companies to be listed among the world's top 100 defence contractors and arms producers. Its defence products increased more than eleven-fold from roughly $1 billion in 2002 to some $11 billion in 2020, and the Turks were able to export more than $3 billion.[47] In spite of their recent accomplishments, however, some ambitious and forward-looking Turkish defence and arms programmes have encountered serious impediments. Turkey simply does not possess certain advanced technologies and technical knowhow to support parts of its high-end and prestigious projects. More importantly, for a whole host of political and security reasons, major Western partners have scaled back their technological cooperation with the Turks, forcing them to approach non-Western arms producers like South Korea for their required technologies and sensitive materials.[48]

A prominent case was the national Altay battle tank project. Turkey began to produce Altay in 2007, but the whole project later hit a snag after Germany refused to supply Turkey with MTU engines and Renk transmissions. The Turkish defence producer, BMC, reportedly had to enter into partnership with two Korean companies, Doosan Infracore and S&T Dynamics, to get its badly needed engine and transmission devices. That is why some reports have asserted that the Turkish Altay is largely based on South Korea's K2 Black Panther tank, although the Turks argue that Altay is an indigenous product.[49] Prior to the Altay case, Turkey had allocated nearly $1 billion from 2004 onwards to import the Korean K9 Thunder technology. After developing the new product, the Turks renamed it the T-155 Fırtına, meaning 'storm'. While the K9 Thunder became one of the most popular South Korean defence items, its Turkish version, T-155 Fırtına, did not achieve the same success and Turkey decided to build only 280 for its own military use.[50]

With regard to developing its own fighter jet programme, Turkey has been compelled to engage in high volumes of arms trading with South Korea over the past two decades. Aiming to replace its ageing US-made T-37 trainer planes with the Korean KT-1Ts, for example, Turkish Aerospace Industries (TAI) signed a $350 million deal with KAI to purchase at least 40 KT-1T basic trainer aircrafts.[51] More recently, a Turkish plan to produce a new generation of fighter jets through cooperation with countries such as Russia has faced strong opposition from its US and European allies. As a matter of fact, both the US and Europe are strongly against any Turkish request to purchase Russian fighter jets for the same reason that a US–EU displeasure with Turkey ultimately bludgeoned Ankara into abandoning a massive $3.4 billion provisional tender in 2013 to purchase a Chinese missile defence

45. SIPRI, *SIPRI Yearbook 2011*, p. 244.
46. Ismail Numan Telci, 'Turkey as a Rising Actor in Global Arms Exports', *Politics Today*, 12 March 2019, <https://www.https://politicstoday.org/turkey-as-a-rising-actor-in-global-arms-exports/>, accessed 17 February 2023.
47. Burak Ege Bekdil, 'Turkey Reports 17% Drop in Defense Exports', *Defense News*, 19 January 2021, <https://www.defensenews.com/global/europe/2021/01/19/turkey-reports-nearly-15-drop-in-defense-exports/>, accessed 17 February 2023.
48. David L Phillips, *An Uncertain Ally: Turkey under Erdogan's Dictatorship* (Abingdon and New York, NY: Routledge, 2017), p. 99–101.
49. Caleb Larson, 'Lookout Syria, Turkey is Building a New Main Battle Tank', *National Interest*, 14 April 2021, <https://nationalinterest.org/blog/buzz/lookout-syria-turkey-building-new-main-battle-tank-182661>, accessed 11 March 2022.
50. Christian F Anrig, 'Turkish Air Power: Toward Full-Spectrum Aerospace Forces', in John Andreas Olsen (ed.), *European Air Power: Challenges and Opportunities* (Sterling, VA: Potomac Books, Inc., 2014), pp. 64–105.
51. *Hürriyet Daily News*, 'Turkey Set to Complete Korea Trainer Plane Program', 16 September 2012, <https://www.hurriyetdailynews.com/turkey-set-to-complete-korea-trainer-plane-program-30291>, accessed 29 April 2023.

system. Such an intractable dilemma may leave the Turks with little option but to turn to South Korea for its 4.5-generation fighter aircraft, known as the KF-21 Boramae.[52]

During the past two decades, therefore, South Korea could ship large cargoes of arms and munitions to Turkey partly because the Turks had to rely on it for several licence-manufactured types of Korean armaments, especially the T-155 howitzer and the K9 Thunder. As a consequence, Turkey was, in terms of volume, the second biggest destination for South Korean exported weapons after Indonesia in the period between 2005 and 2009.[53] From 2010 until 2014, only seven countries in the world received South Korea's defence products, but almost half of those Korean exported arms ended up in Turkey. In 2016–2017, the Turks stood out as the biggest recipient of South Korea's weapons and military goods, and continued to bring in a significant volume of Korean defence products from 2018 onward.[54] South Korea's recent success in signing a number of high-value arms deals with other Middle Eastern countries, the United Arab Emirates (UAE) in particular, may overshadow Turkey's position as a prominent importer of South Korean armaments in the region for the past two decades. However, in all likelihood, Ankara will be tempted to maintain its growing defence cooperation with Seoul now that the Turks are more dependent than ever on the South Koreans to advance some of their ambitious military plans, such as the fifth-generation fighter jet project.

Table 2: Global Share of Top Middle Eastern Importers of Arms, 2017–20

Country	Percentage share
Saudi Arabia	11
Egypt	5.7
Qatar	4.6
UAE	2.8

Source: SIPRI, *SIPRI Yearbook 2021*.

The GCC in the Crosshairs: Setting a New Record in the UAE

Since its creation in the early 1980s, the Gulf Cooperation Council (GCC) has been in the limelight of global arms producers as its relatively wealthy Arab members have often been among the world's top customers of expensive weapons and sophisticated defence products. From Americans to Europeans and from Russians to Chinese, almost all major merchants of armaments in the world have constantly strived to capture a larger share of the GCC's seemingly bottomless pit of weapons procurements.[55] While an international rivalry for the GCC's arms markets is heating up, South Korean defence companies have been willing to cater to increasing demands from deep-pocketed Arab states by offering them their diversified products, ranging from tear gas to cluster bombs, and battle tanks to fighter jets. The South Koreans have also strived to pitch their defence products throughout the GCC, seeing the greatest success in fostering defence interactions and selling arms to Oman, Saudi Arabia and particularly the UAE.[56]

The relatively conservative and cautious Sultanate of Oman was not sought after by the major Western and Eastern merchants of armaments in the past, but it has tried in recent years to boost its defence capabilities by spending billions of dollars on arms imports. In 2021, Oman positioned itself as the world's 38th top country in terms of military expenditure by allocating some $5.8 billion or 7.3% (the highest in the world) of its GDP on arms and defence affairs.[57] A great deal of Oman's imported weapons normally come from Western markets, but the Sultanate has also paid attention to some non-Western suppliers of arms, including South Korea. The largest reported deal involving arms transactions between Oman and Korea took place in late 2018 when the GCC state signed an agreement worth around $885 million to purchase 76 K2 Black Panthers – South Korea's main battle tank produced by Hyundai Rotem Corporation. In addition to negotiating a number of other low-key arms deals between the Sultanate and South Korea

52. Paul Iddon, 'Will Turkey Seek Chinese or Korean Fighters if F-16 Request is Denied?', *Forbes*, 23 January 2022.
53. *SIPRI Yearbook 2011*, p. 242.
54. Ferhat Gurini, 'Turkey's Unpromising Defense Industry', Carnegie Endowment for International Peace, 9 October 2020, <https://carnegieendowment.org/sada/82936>, accessed 21 December 2022.
55. Raphael Israeli, *From Arab Spring to Islamic Winter* (New Brunswick, NJ: Transaction Publishers, 2013), p. 128.
56. Sehun Cheon and Joonsoo Park, 'Is South Korea's Booming Defence Industry Here to Stay?', *East Asia Forum*, 14 December 2022, <https://www.eastasiaforum.org/2022/12/14/is-south-koreas-booming-defence-industry-here-to-stay/>, accessed 19 February 2023.
57. SIPRI, *SIPRI Fact Sheet*, pp. 2, 9.

over the past several years, top defence and military officials from the two countries have exchanged several official visits with the aim of enhancing their bilateral relationship in this critical area.[58]

In comparison with Oman, the kingdom of Saudi Arabia has long been one of the world's top purchaser of almost any type of weapons, allocating more than $55 billion (6.6%) of its GDP on military expenditure in 2021 alone. Under the Saudi Vision 2030,[59] moreover, this GCC heavyweight has aimed ambitiously to produce at least half of its defence requirements domestically in the coming years. This was a major reason why, in early July 2019, the Saudis signed a memorandum of understanding (MoU) with three affiliate companies of South Korea's Hanwha Group, to set up a joint venture company in Saudi Arabia to manufacture military products.[60] The South Koreans subsequently increased their efforts to promote their military products among the Saudis after they managed to secure a lucrative arms deal worth $989 million in March 2022, to sell various types of ammunition supplied by three South Korean defence companies: Hanwha, Poongsan and LIG Nex1.[61] The two sides have recently vowed to 'drastically bolster' their bilateral partnership in different areas including defence, prompting the Koreans to pitch their more expensive and advanced weapons to the Saudis, such as Biho-II, an anti-aircraft defence system, and the Cheongung-II mid-range surface-to-air missile (SAM).[62]

In the face of South Korea's relentless quest for engaging in arms deals and defence cooperation with Oman and Saudi Arabia over the past several years, however, its watershed moment in the regional Arab bloc occurred in the UAE in early 2022, more than a decade after South Korea had signed an unusual contract to build four nuclear reactors for the Emiratis.[63] In December 2009, when a South Korean consortium led by the Korean Electronic Power Company (KEPCO) won a jackpot contract of roughly $20 billion to construct nuclear plants for the UAE, the bilateral deal turned out to be far beyond normal business, including transfer of South Korea's sensitive nuclear knowhow. The nuclear power agreement soon involved an undisclosed military deal between the Koreans and the Emiratis, which did not require approval by the South Korean National Assembly. As an outcome of that secretive pact, from early 2011 onward, South Korea sent on a rotational basis, hundreds of its military forces to the UAE to conduct joint military exercises and participate in various defence exchanges with their Emirati counterparts.[64] Such developments contributed to the so-called 'strategic partnership' and security interactions between South Korea and the UAE, facilitating South Korea's defence industry to achieve the pinnacle of its export success by winning over the Emiratis to purchase its advanced missile interceptor.

In January 2022, three Korean defence companies, LIG Nex1, Hanwha Defense, and Hanwha Systems, signed an unprecedented deal worth 4 trillion won ($3.22 billion) to sell its mid-range surface-to-air missile (KM-SAM), known as Cheongung-II, to the UAE.[65] Apart from being the largest foreign order in the history of the Korean defence industry, the bankable agreement marked the first time South Korea could sell its multi-layered anti-missile system to another country. It was only in 2010 when Korea's defence industry dreamed of materialising export revenues of about $4 billion by 2020, but South Korea could now make something close to that figure by agreeing to supply its KM-SAM to a single

58. *Yonhap News Agency*, 'S. Korean, Omani Defense Chiefs Agree to Strengthen Cooperation', 2 September 2021, <https://en.yna.co.kr/view/AEN20210902003200325>, accessed 20 February 2023.
59. For further information, see <https://www.vision2030.gov.sa/>.
60. *Middle East Monitor*, 'Saudi Arabia, South Korea Sign Arms Manufacture Deal', 2 July 2019, <https://www.middleeastmonitor.com/20190702-saudi-arabia-south-korea-sign-mou-for-a-joint-venture/>, accessed 20 February 2023.
61. Kyung-Min Kang, 'Hanwha, Poongsan, LIG Nex1 Clinch $989 mn Saudi Defense Deals', *KED Global*, 10 March 2022, <https://www.kedglobal.com/aerospace-defense/newsView/ked202203100011>, accessed 11 January 2023.
62. Irang Bak, 'Saudi Arabia and South Korea "Drastically" Deepen Ties after Crown Prince Visit', *Middle East Eye*, 27 November 2022, <https://www.middleeasteye.net/news/saudi-arabia-south-korea-deepen-ties-crown-prince-visit>, accessed 21 February 2023.
63. Mark Episkopos, 'South Korea Inks Record Missile Deal with the UAE', *National Interest*, 20 January 2022, <https://nationalinterest.org/blog/buzz/south-korea-inks-record-missile-deal-uae-199705>, accessed 23 February 2022.
64. Shirzad Azad, 'Bidding for a Place in the Sun: The Looking-East Policy of the United Arab Emirates', *Contemporary Arab Affairs* (Vol. 13, No. 4, December 2020), pp. 70–87.
65. Nam Hyun-woo, 'Yoon Kicks off UAE Visit to Promote Power Plant, Arms Exports', *Korea Times*, 15 January 2023, <https://www.koreatimes.co.kr/www/common/printpreviews.asp?categoryCode=356&newsIdx=343593>, accessed 20 February 2023.

Table 3: The Top Seven Countries in the Middle East with the Largest Military Expenditure, 2021

Country	Military spending, $ billion	Military expenditure as a percentage share of GDP
Saudi Arabia	55.6	6.6
Iran	24.6	2.3
Israel	24.3	5.2
Turkey	15.5	2.1
Qatar	11.6	4.8
Kuwait	9	6.7
Oman	5.8	7.3

Source: SIPRI, 'SIPRI Fact Sheet: Trends in World Military Expenditure, 2021', April 2022, <https://www.sipri.org/sites/default/files/2022-04/fs_2204_milex_2021_0.pdf>, accessed 29 April 2023.

foreign customer alone.[66] The two sides did not disclose any information concerning the delivery time of the Cheongung-II missile system, which can intercept both ballistic missiles and aircrafts, but a number of UAE neighbours, Iran in particular, quickly expressed their displeasure with the sale of this sophisticated Korean weapon to the tumultuous and conflict-prone region of the Middle East.[67]

Embracing Egypt: Straddling Middle Eastern and North African Arms Markets

Although South Korea has just started to develop its arms deals with Egypt, the Egyptian government has long had close military and defence interactions with the Korean Peninsula, harking back to the early 1970s, when North Korea sent its pilots to help the Middle Eastern country and its Arab allies fight their 1973 war against Israel.[68] In the following decades, Cairo and Pyongyang maintained their military and defence relationship, including missile cooperation, even after Egypt made peace with Israel and subsequently became a major recipient of various Western military aids and weapons. It was in summer 2016 when an Egypt-bound North Korean ship, *Jie Shun*, was caught carrying 30,000 rocket-propelled grenades, valued at more than $25 million. The incident, which led the US to cut or suspend, albeit temporarily, some of its military aids to Egypt because of international sanctions violations against Pyongyang, forced the Egyptian government to end its military connections with North Korea for the time being.[69]

Halfway through the *Jie Shun* controversy, however, South Korean officials were negotiating with their Egyptian counterparts over the export of the Korean K-9 self-propelled howitzers. In fact, as early as 2010, South Korea was courting Egypt over the sale of its K-9 howitzers, but the Egyptian government was soon engulfed by the Arab Uprising, which curtailed procurement for the Korean weapon by Cairo.[70] It took several years before the new military rulers of Egypt were willing to renew their stalled talks with Seoul to purchase the Korean K-9 artillery. At the same time, post-crisis Egypt went on a defence spending spree, engaging in massive arms deals with major armaments producers from the West and the East. This was another reason that compelled the Korean government to curry favour with new Egyptian rulers concerning the impending bilateral agreement over the export of K-9 to Cairo. As a major importer of arms and munitions, Egypt had been a focus of the Korean defence industry for many years, and the sale of K-9 Thunder could turn the Arab country into one of the up-and-coming

66. Nam Hyun-woo, 'Korea Signs W4 Tril. Export Deal with UAE for Cheongung-II Missile System', *Korea Times*, 17 January 2022, <https://www.koreatimes.co.kr/www/nation/2022/01/205_322373.html>, accessed 9 April 2022.
67. Frank Smith, 'South Korea's UAE Weapons Deal Draws Criticism', *Press TV*, 24 January 2022, <https://www.presstv.ir/Detail/2022/01/24/675449/South-Korea's-UAE-weapons-deal-draws-criticism>, accessed 1 March 2022.
68. Robert A Scalapino and Hongkoo Lee (eds.), *North Korea in a Regional and Global Context* (Berkeley, CA: University of California, Berkeley, Center for Korean Studies, 1986), p. 338.
69. Declan Walsh, 'Need a North Korean Missile? Call the Cairo Embassy', *New York Times*, 3 March 2018.
70. Kang Hyun-kyung, 'Korean Investment in Egypt Unswayed by Arab Spring', *Korea Times*, 31 May 2015, <https://www.koreatimes.co.kr/www/news/nation/2015/05/ 176_179886.html>, accessed 19 November 2022.

Table 4: Major Arms Deals Between South Korea and Middle Eastern Countries, 2004–22

ME country	Year	Value of deal	Type of weapon
Egypt	2022	$1.65 billion	K-9 howitzer
Iraq	2013–14	$2.1 billion	T-50 fighter jet
Oman	2018	$884.6 million	K2 Black Panther
Saudi Arabia	2022	$989 million	Various types of ammunition
Turkey	2004–20	Upwards of $1 billion	K9 Thunder, KT-1T aircraft, T-155 howitzer
UAE	2022	$3.22 billion	Cheongung-II missile system

Source: The Author (collated data from sources included in this article).

markets for its arms shipment to the greater Middle East region, including North Africa.[71]

After more than a decade of negotiations, therefore, in early February 2022, South Korea and Egypt signed a $1.65 billion deal to trade the Hanwha Defense-manufactured K-9 howitzers. The lucrative agreement, which was the single biggest sale of K-9 to a foreign country, opened a new chapter in South Korea's defense industry, coming after South Korea was able to sell successfully its K-9 howitzers to seven other nations, including Turkey, India, Poland, Estonia, Finland, Norway and Australia. The defence contract made it possible for South Korea to export, for the first time, its K-9 howitzers to a country located in Africa, setting the Korean defence industry in motion to look for more new customers across the continent for the howitzers and other arms products. This ambition was further enabled because the agreement with Egypt involved the transfer of technology to – and the production of K-9 howitzers in – Egypt, paving the way for it to act as an outpost to sell Korean weapons to other African countries.[72]

Conclusion

After decades of uninterrupted investments, and benefiting enormously from US training and technology, South Korea's defence industry has emerged among the world's leading producers and exporters of arms and munitions. Exporting various types of defence products worth roughly $17 billion in 2022 alone, South Korea has set the highly ambitious goal of becoming one of the world's top four merchants of armaments by 2027.[73] To advance its military programmes, and make more pecuniary gains from its enhanced defence technologies, South Korea has attempted unflinchingly to seize a larger share of the global arms markets by making inroads into almost every promising region which is going to import weapons for the foreseeable future. The greater Middle East region, including North Africa, has been one of those up-and-coming parts of the world that has recently become a rendezvous of major Korean defence companies, although the early history of South Korea's arms deals with the Middle East goes back to the Iran–Iraq War in the 1980s, during which it engaged in intermittent and covert arms business with both sides.

In the 1980s, South Korea was still an underdeveloped and unknown player in the world markets of armaments, and the South Koreans were more famous for their export of manpower to the Middle East, carrying out numerous construction projects throughout the region. Although Middle Eastern nations continued to receive large cargoes of foreign weapons and defence products, South Korea's military industrial complex still needed several more decades to develop before making a comeback by signing dozens of profitable arms deals with many countries across the region. During those decades, however, South Korea's swiftly growing industrial and technological power enabled various

71. Kim Deok-hyun, 'Moon, Egyptian Leader to Make Joint Efforts for K-9 Howitzer Deal', *Yonhap News Agency*, 20 January 2022, <https://en.yna.co.kr/view/AEN20220120009551315>, accessed 16 December 2022.
72. Song Sang-ho and Kang Yoon-seung, 'S. Korea to Export K9 Howitzers to Egypt in 2 Tln Won Deal', *Yonhap News Agency*, 1 February 2022, <https://en.yna.co.kr/view/AEN20220201001900325>, accessed 11 March 2022.
73. Dasl Yoon, 'Ukraine War Drives Rapid Growth in South Korea's Arms Exports', *Wall Street Journal*, 2 February 2023.

South Korean brands and manufactured goods to gradually capture a substantial share of the Middle East's bankable imports markets. Major Korean companies could also become important investment and technological partners of Middle Eastern countries, persuading them over time to bargain for more sensitive Korean products such as nuclear power technology and state-of-the-art armaments.

A last, but significant, factor contributing to South Korea's growing arms trade with the Middle East is that major arms customers in the region have increasingly carved out their own ambitious defence projects to produce more weapons domestically in the hopes of achieving self-sufficiency and becoming a credible merchant of armaments one day. As well as a number of Turkish defence contractors, and the Emirati EDGE Group, hoping to make it onto the list of the world's top arms-producing companies, Egypt is also pushing to manufacture a higher volume of its required weapons at home, with the prospect of exporting part of its defence products in the future. As these countries still lag behind South Korea both in terms of arms technology and research, they would have a better chance of achieving their long-term objectives through the purchase of South Korea's advanced weaponry, and entering into joint partnership with Korean defence companies. ■

Shirzad Azad is Associate Professor of International Relations in the Department of Political Science at Ferdowsi University of Mashhad, Iran. His previous works have been published in several peer-reviewed journals, including *Middle East Policy*, *The International Spectator*, *Asian Affairs*, *Contemporary Arab Affairs*, *Asian Politics and Policy*, *Contemporary Review of the Middle East*, and *East Asia: An International Quarterly*.

Research Article
RUSI Journal

The International Legion of Ukraine

Exploring the Background and Motivations of Foreign Volunteers

Matteo Pugliese

In the aftermath of Russia's full-scale invasion of Ukraine in February 2022, President Volodymyr Zelensky established an International Legion and thousands of foreign volunteers came to defend the country. Matteo Pugliese examines the structure of the Legion, its recruitment process, the volunteers' origin and their reasons to enlist. Relying on conversations and interviews carried out in July 2022 at the Legion's premises and in other locations across Ukraine, he argues that the Legion represents only a small portion of Ukraine's foreign volunteers, who came mainly from the West and Latin America with a diverse set of backgrounds and motivations.

Following the full-scale invasion of Ukraine in February 2022, thousands of volunteers from abroad began flowing in to help repel the Russian occupants. This raised increasing concerns about their role, with Russian propaganda depicting them as neo-Nazi militants, associated with the Azov regiment or other extremist groups.[1] International media seldom emphasises the divide between the first generation of foreign volunteers (2014–15), motivated by far-right ideology in a radicalisation process,[2] and the current wave, which is driven by different push and pull factors.

Aware of the composite network of Ukraine's volunteer units (Belarusian regiments, the Georgian National Legion,[3] Free Russia Legion, Russian Volunteer Corps, Chechen battalions, among others), this article focuses solely on the International Legion of Defence of Ukraine (hereinafter 'the Legion' or 'the International Legion') and explores the personal and political background of volunteers, as well as their motivations to enlist. It also provides an account of the International Legion's operational framework, group dynamics and some security implications in the long term. The research aims to address these issues by analysing the Legion's structure and recruitment process.

Between July 2022 and January 2023, the author reached out to 19 foreign volunteers who joined the Ukrainian ranks. The conversations were held first in person during the fieldwork in Ukraine and in the following months by phone and online. All interviewees have been informed about the author's research purpose aimed at exploring the motivations and profiles of foreign volunteers. Two admitted having fought in Ukraine but did not provide further details about their deployment, while the author conducted a series of interviews and follow-ups with the remaining pool of volunteers, which offered a significant amount of information regarding their background and personal data, experience on the

1. The Soufan Center, 'Foreign Fighters, Volunteers, and Mercenaries: Non-State Actors and Narratives in Ukraine', 4 April 2022, <https://thesoufancenter.org/research/foreign-fighters-volunteers-and-mercenaries-non-state-actors-and-narratives-in-ukraine/>, accessed 13 April 2023.
2. Alex MacKenzie and Christian Kaunert, 'Radicalisation, Foreign Fighters and the Ukraine Conflict: A Playground for the Far-Right?', *Social Sciences* (Vol. 10, No. 4, March 2021), p. 116. DOI: https://doi.org/10.3390/socsci10040116.
3. Adam Potočňák and Miroslav Mareš, 'Georgian Foreign Fighters in the Conflict in Eastern Ukraine 2014–2017', *Journal of Slavic Military Studies* (Vol. 32, No. 2, 2019), pp. 159–77.

An International Legion of Ukraine foreign volunteer soldier at Kyiv Central Train Station, February 2023. *Courtesy of Kish Kim / Sipa US / Alamy*

battlefield and views on the conflict. The author also monitored the foreign volunteers' community on two social networks (Instagram and Facebook), gathering further information on the connections of its members, geographical origin and political ideas.

The interviewees' anonymity was preserved throughout the whole research process and their identity shall not be disclosed. Foreign volunteers and, more generally, soldiers from the Armed Forces of Ukraine are not allowed to disclose details about the Legion and the military for obvious operational security reasons and could be severely punished under martial law. Given the security context in which the research was carried out and considering the serious allegations of threats and violence perpetrated by some officers of the Legion (GUR wing) against volunteers, the author anonymised all interviewees.

The author applied a semi-structured interview methodology for some of the volunteers and an unstructured method for others, based on the security context and their role. This methodology helped significantly to put at ease the respondents, without rigid and prearranged questions that may have either prevented or influenced their answers, especially when it comes to controversial issues and internal dynamics. When foreign volunteers are explicitly named, this is always in relation to public statements to the press or on social media, never for comments given during interviews and conversations with the author.

The Legion's Functioning and Its Impact on Volunteers

The Evolution and Structure of the Legion

The creation of the International Legion of Defence of Ukraine was announced on 27 February 2022 by President Volodymyr Zelensky, five days after the full-scale Russian invasion.[4] Since then, the Legion has been shaped by a number of events, but the main turning point was the 13 March 2022 Russian strike on the International Peacekeeping and Security Centre in Yavoriv, western Ukraine. In early March, the Ukrainian Defence Ministry stated

4. Pavel Polityuk, 'Ukraine Establishing Foreign Legion for Volunteers from Abroad – President', *Reuters*, 27 February 2022.

that over 20,000 volunteers from 52 countries had applied to join the International Legion,[5] and at least 1,000 of them had already reached the recruitment and training hub in Yavoriv.[6] When the Russian cruise missiles hit the centre on 13 March, Kyiv's authorities acknowledged dozens of Ukrainian losses, but the Legion repeatedly confirmed 'with absolute certainty that no [foreign] recruits lost their lives in this attack'.[7] However, the shock pushed thousands of them to quit and leave the country.[8] A Polish veteran of Afghanistan, who enlisted with the Legion, commented that the attack was 'the best selection of the people that you could imagine',[9] because those without any war experience understood they were not fit for the job.

Given the amateurish performance of volunteers from the initial intake on the battlefield,[10] and the mass exodus in the aftermath of the Yavoriv strike, Ukrainian generals demanded a review of the recruitment criteria and some senior officers even asked to disband the Legion altogether,[11] and eventually obtained it to be limited to candidates with previous combat experience. The government imposed stricter rules, although the vetting process was not always effective and compliant with them. The following cohort of recruits appears more skilled and prepared. For instance, the whole group of Latin American volunteers engaged by the author holds previous military experience.[12]

As of August 2022, the International Legion consisted of an infantry battalion with three companies: Alpha, Bravo and Charlie with, according to estimates, up to 250 active members.[13] Until the summer, the acting commander of the Legion was Major Bogdan Molchanov, an officer from the Ukrainian armed forces.[14] From May until the counteroffensive in September 2022, companies Bravo and Charlie defended entrenched positions on the west bank of the Donets river, between the Staryi Saltiv and Molodova villages in the Kharkiv oblast,[15] with the second line held by Pravyi Sektor's Ukrainian Volunteer Corps.[16] But elements of the

5. Government of Ukraine, 'Stvoreno spetspidrozdil Internatsional'noho lehionu pry HUR MO Ukrayiny, vin vzhe vykonuye boyovi zavdannya' ['A Special Unit of the International Legion was Created under the GUR of the Ministry of Defense of Ukraine, and it is Already Performing Combat Tasks'], 7 March 2022, <https://gur.gov.ua/content/stvoreno-spetspidrozdil-internatsionalnoho-lehionu-pry-hur-mo-ukrainy-vin-vzhe-vykonuie-boiovi-zavdannia.html>, accessed 13 April 2023.
6. Austin Ramzy, 'The Base Attacked in Western Ukraine has been a Hub for Foreign Militaries', *New York Times*, 13 March 2022.
7. International Legion's official Facebook page, post, 16 March 2022, <https://www.facebook.com/ukr.international.legion/posts/pfbid02MJq3tUWmUwhQKVfThkoNV35Cb14HW3Jcic6vS5a9xwQN5ii3ay1iw9ytrEtc6Feol>, accessed 13 April 2023.
8. Tim Hume, '"I Don't Want to be Cannon Fodder": Foreign Fighters are Leaving Ukraine', *Vice News*, 30 March 2022, <https://www.vice.com/en/article/akv898/foreign-fighters-quit-ukraine>, accessed 13 April 2023.
9. Alastair McCready, 'Returning Soldiers Reveal the Dark Side of Life in the Ukrainian Foreign Legion', *Vice News*, 29 March 2022, <https://www.vice.com/en/article/y3v4xj/joining-ukrainian-foreign-legion>, accessed 13 April 2023.
10. Andrew Milburn, 'Legion of the Damned: Inside Ukraine's Army of Misfits, Veterans, and War Tourists in the Fight Against Russia', *Task and Purpose*, 18 March 2022, <https://taskandpurpose.com/news/ukraine-foreign-legion/>, accessed 13 April 2023.
11. Author interview with a Legion staffer, Ukraine, July 2022.
12. Data and resumes of 10 Latin American volunteers shared with the author, August 2022.
13. Author conversation with former legionnaires deployed to the frontline, Ukraine, July 2022.
14. Several official documents are signed by Major Bogdan Molchanov as acting commander of the International Legion. See, for instance, Lucia Landoni, 'Benjamin Giorgio Galli morto a 27 anni in Ucraina: chi è il foreign fighter. La madre: "Si sentiva nel posto giusto"' ['Benjamin Giorgio Galli Died at 27 in Ukraine: Who is the Foreign Fighter. Mother: "He Felt in the Right Place"'], *La Repubblica*, 20 September 2022, <https://milano.repubblica.it/cronaca/2022/09/20/news/giorgio_galli_italiano_morto_ucraina_foreign_fighter-366512043?>, accessed 13 April 2023; see also: Nic White and Daniel Piotrowski, 'Australia's The Block "Conwoman" Bizarrely Resurfaces in Ukraine where She is Fighting Russians under the Codename "Mockingjay" and Posing with an Assault Rifle - After Sparking Chaos on a Remote Tropical Island', *Daily Mail*, 13 July 2022.
15. Author conversation with former legionnaires deployed in Molodova, Ukraine, July 2022. Following the September counteroffensive, the frontline advanced several kilometers and in terms of operational security was safe to disclose the former location of the Ukrainian positions.
16. See Facebook post of Viktor Serdulets alias Roman Zhakhiv, 'Роман Жахів' (far-right activist and commander of Pravyi Sektor's militia 'Tryzub', senior sergeant in the Ukrainian Ground Forces), with an American volunteer and a Canadian volunteer, 12 May 2022, <https://www.facebook.com/novelofhorror/posts/pfbid0Ldybm5BdMXCV9ivoiF2TDvh1mfZxa8Edip8WNVWWtnxrg8ecPrn3is7kXK54Nc5zl>, accessed 13 April 2023; a Ukrainian serviceman and French foreign legion soldier, operating with the GUR wing of the Ukrainian Legion, shared on social media posts from Pravyi Sektor's Volunteer Corps in which they ask for funds for their unit.

Legion were deployed in many sectors across Ukraine.[17] In addition, since 27 February 2022 Ukraine's military intelligence has been recruiting foreigners from the Legion's pool for a separate unit, which operates directly under its command and control.[18]

In September 2022, the Legion established a 3rd Battalion under the command of the Ground Forces, although some smaller units were embedded by GUR (military intelligence) officers, and during winter a 2nd Battalion was being set up as well.[19] This means the total number of enlisted and trained volunteers increased over the months. It is common to give military units numbers that do not correspond to the actual size of the force, and also to disorientate the enemy's assessment of the force.

Foreigners can allegedly receive only enlisted ranks (corporal), regardless of their previous senior military rank.[20] That is why Charlie company, for instance, was commanded by a Ukrainian captain named Taras, assisted by a Ukrainian non-commissioned officer as a deputy, while Bravo company was led by a Norwegian-Ukrainian dual national, who could therefore be appointed as a commander.[21] Platoon leaders are foreigners though, and Latin American fighters were gathered into the 1st platoon of Charlie company, while Anglo-Saxon volunteers were mostly in the 3rd platoon.[22]

Some legionnaires expressed frustration at being enlisted as privates or corporals, having held a rank of commissioned officer in their country of origin.[23] A retired colonel from the British Army that enlisted in the Legion was reportedly ordered to take picket at the trenches.[24] Other foreign senior officers seem fine with being demoted to the rank of private. For instance, a retired full colonel from the Canadian Army, with 36 years of service including in Somalia, Bosnia and Afghanistan, said he has 'confidence in the Ukrainian leadership in the Legion and know[s] they are doing their utmost to put our skills to best use on the front'.[25]

The Legion's support staff, based in Kyiv, in 2022 amounted to three–four individuals only. The staff included the French-Norwegian spokesperson Damien Magrou, who resigned on 8 September 2022,[26] the Hungarian communication officer Emese Fajk, aka Abigel Fuchs, and the Czech logistics director known as 'Santa'. None of them had previous military experience whatsoever. Magrou is an international lawyer who was already living in Ukraine before the invasion and 'Santa' was a mortgage manager from the Czech Republic who decided to travel to Ukraine after President Zelensky's plea.[27] In mid-July, media reports emerged about Fajk's past, as she fled Australia in 2020 after reportedly being exposed using fake bank slips for $4.2 million to win the reality TV show *The Block*.[28] Fajk later settled in the Portuguese island of Madeira with the identity of Abigel Fuchs, but she was accused by two different former boyfriends

17. Joe Duggan, 'Ukraine War: Injured British Fighter Paraded on Russian State Television Asking "Am I Safe?"', *INews*, 30 April 2022, <https://inews.co.uk/news/world/ukraine-war-injured-british-fighter-russian-state-television-1604518>, accessed 13 April 2023.
18. Christopher Miller, 'A Team of American and British Special Forces Veterans are Preparing to Join Ukraine's Fight Against Russia', *BuzzFeed News*, 27 February 2022, <https://www.buzzfeednews.com/article/christopherm51/american-nato-military-veterans-fight-russia-with-ukraine>, accessed 13 April 2023.
19. Author conversation with a former Legion staffer, December 2022.
20. Author conversation with a former legionnaire deployed to the frontline, Ukraine, July 2022.
21. Author conversation with legionnaires, Ukraine, July 2022.
22. Author conversation with a former legionnaire deployed to the frontline, Ukraine, July 2022.
23. Author interview with legionnaires, Ukraine, July 2022.
24. Author conversation with a former legionnaire deployed to the frontline, Ukraine, July 2022.
25. International Legion's official Facebook page, post, 11 April 2022, <https://www.facebook.com/ukr.international.legion/posts/pfbid02SmKd159oTcCYzVgxKzQMJrqm2ugSyq1NoF9DWCzuVL4Cpt1EnD6mWs6VJCKjBjw5l>, accessed 13 April 2023.
26. Damien Magrou's LinkedIn post, 13 September 2022, <https://www.linkedin.com/posts/damienmagrou_hi-everyone-i-have-several-announcements-activity-6975118976657805312-6tnB?utm_source=share&utm_medium=member_desktop>, accessed 13 April 2023.
27. Author interview with a Legion staffer, Ukraine, July 2022.
28. Daniel Piotrowski, 'How *The Block*'s "International Conwoman" Appears to be Up to her Old Tricks after Fleeing to a Remote Island Off Portugal to "Hide from her Problems" – As she's Chased by her Landlord for Rent and Accused of Doctoring Bank Slips', *Daily Mail*, 26 April 2021.

and her landlord of being a fraudster and sending fake proof of payment for rent.[29] She suddenly left Madeira and signed a contract with the Legion on 8 April 2022, becoming the communication officer.

The Legion's GUR Wing

On 17 August 2022, the *Kyiv Independent* published an in-depth investigation on the alleged abuse of power in the GUR wing of the Legion. A group of legionnaires submitted a 78-page report about their commanders' misconduct to Ukrainian law enforcement and institutions.[30] Reportedly, the GUR wing of the Legion was coordinated by four people: major Vadym Popyk, intelligence major Taras Vashuk, his uncle (referred to as 'old Taras'), and 60-year-old Sasha Kuchynsky.[31] Members of the unit accused the two Taras of sending soldiers on suicide missions. A former member of the Legion's GUR wing provided the same feedback to the author and mentioned lack of discipline and suicide missions as the main reasons why he quit.[32] Another former legionnaire described the special GUR wing of the Legion as 'not-so-special', referring to lack of professionalism and safety protocols.

The *Kyiv Independent* disclosed the identity of the GUR officer known as Sasha Kuchynsky: he is a Polish former member of the Pruszków mafia group and his real name is Piotr Kapuscinski aka 'Broda' (Beard). He avoided at least 71 charges in Poland, including kidnapping for ransom, by cooperating with law enforcement as a 'crown witness' in 2009.[33] Kapuscinski fled Poland in 2014 and in 2016 was investigated in Ukraine for aggravated robbery and sexual assault, but was only charged with robbery, the *Kyiv Independent* reported.[34] In November 2016, he was detained in Ukraine and spent over a year in prison, while in 2021 police investigated him for illegal possession of weapons and explosives, but this did not prevent him from getting enlisted into the Legion as a field commander. According to legionnaires' testimonies and photographs, Kapuscinski calls himself a colonel and wears a colonel's epaulet, but he is a non-commissioned officer. Kapuscinski is accused of threatening an American volunteer with a gun as well as of looting a shopping mall in Severodonetsk, a video published by the *Kyiv Independent* shows.[35] These and other serious allegations were submitted to the military prosecutor who is investigating the case.[36] An American volunteer commented that 'people like Sasha really discredit all of this',[37] referring to the Legion's effort in the war.

In September 2022, an entire unit of 11 volunteers from Colombia, Chile, Argentina and Italy who joined the GUR wing of the Legion in August was discharged due to the language barrier with Spanish speakers, but allegedly also for a sort of discrimination against Latinos from one of the

29. Rohan Smith, 'Alleged Block Conwoman Emese Fajk Blasts Critics Accusing her of "War PR" as she Fights for Ukraine', *News.com.au*, 15 July 2022, <https://www.news.com.au/entertainment/tv/reality-tv/alleged-block-conwoman-emese-fajk-holds-press-conference-in-wartorn-ukraine/news-story/ec15ddc8d014ffdd6148e71ffaac1048>, accessed 13 April 2023.
30. Anna Myroniuk and Alexander Khrebet, 'Suicide Missions, Abuse, Physical Threats: International Legion Fighters Speak Out Against Leadership's Misconduct', *Kyiv Independent*, 17 August 2022, <https://kyivindependent.com/investigations/suicide-missions-abuse-physical-threats-international-legion-fighters-speak-out-against-leaderships-misconduct>, accessed 13 April 2023.
31. *Ibid*.
32. Author conversation with a former member of the GUR wing of the Legion, Ukraine, July 2022.
33. Izabela Kacprzak and Grazyna Zawadka, 'Dlaczego zwlekano z odebraniem statusu świadka koronnego "Brodzie"' ['Why was the Decision to Terminate "Broda's" Witness Protection Delayed?'], *Rzeczpospolita*, 27 February 2020, <https://www.rp.pl/przestepczosc/art9032711-dlaczego-zwlekano-z-odebraniem-statusu-swiadka-koronnego-brodzie>, accessed 13 April 2023.
34. Myroniuk and Khrebet, 'Suicide Missions, Abuse, Physical Threats: International Legion Fighters Speak Out Against Leadership's Misconduct'.
35. Video on *Kyiv Independent*'s Youtube channel, 'International Legion fighters claim their commander ordered them to steal goods from a shopping mall', YouTube, <https://www.youtube.com/watch?v=YZ1zsW8JnMA&ab_channel=KyivIndependent>, accessed 13 April 2023.
36. Anna Myroniuk and Alexander Khrebet, 'Investigation: International Legion Soldiers Allege Light Weapons Misappropriation, Abuse by Commanders', *Kyiv Independent*, 30 November 2022, <https://kyivindependent.com/investigation-international-legion-misappropriation/>, accessed 13 April 2023.
37. Myroniuk and Khrebet, 'Suicide Missions, Abuse, Physical Threats: International Legion Fighters Speak Out Against Leadership's Misconduct'.

GUR commanders.[38] These volunteers from Latin American countries were not deployed despite documented previous military experience and were instead used for pointless tasks, like painting fences in Ternopil.[39]

In September 2022, a new GUR wing unit was established and included Anglophone volunteers such as US Navy veteran and MSNBC pundit Malcolm Nance,[40] as well as some of the previously discharged Latin American volunteers, including two paramedics.[41] Major Bogdan Molchakov, previously leader of the 1st Battalion of the Legion,[42] was promoted to lieutenant colonel and appointed as the new commander of this unit,[43] which was deployed for reconnaissance missions on the Lugansk oblast frontline, between Kupiansk and Svatove in late October and early November, suffering casualties due to heavy artillery fire,[44] but also capturing a Russian prisoner of war.[45] Following the losses, many members of this unit decided to quit and leave Ukraine.[46]

The Legion and the GUR wing have different social media accounts on Instagram,[47] while on Twitter there is only one of the 'ordinary' Legion, and on Facebook there are two pages actively posting content, but only one received the blue badge as a verified account.[48] On Instagram, a unit belonging to the GUR wing called 'Black Team', with at least 15 members, has its own account and displays as its logo an Icelandic magical symbol known as *Vegvísir*, encircled by runic letters.[49] The Black Team was deployed in the Kherson oblast on naval warfare operations alongside Ukrainian Special Forces, but also in Donbas.[50]

The International Legion suffered heavy casualties, mostly due to artillery strikes on Ukrainian positions. During the most intense phase of the fighting in Donbas, the casualty rate reportedly reached dramatic levels, around 50% among the recruits sent to the frontline.[51] The heavy death toll, often caused by artillery strikes, had a serious psychological impact on volunteers. Some of them, following the traumatic death of a comrade in arms, bought vodka bottles from Molodova villagers (despite the platoon leader asking them not to sell it), and were discharged by the company commander for drinking on duty.[52]

The Recruitment and Vetting Process of the Legion

On 5 March the Ukrainian government launched a website (fightforua.org) for those wishing to join

38. Author conversation with members of the GUR wing of the Legion, September 2022.
39. Author conversation with members of the GUR wing of the Legion, September 2022.
40. Nardine Saad, 'Former MSNBC Analyst Malcolm Nance Join's the Fight in Ukraine "I'm Done Talking"', *LA Times*, 19 April 2022, <https://www.latimes.com/entertainment-arts/tv/story/2022-04-19/former-msnbc-analyst-malcolm-nance-joins-fight-in-ukraine-im-done-talking>, accessed 3 May 2023.
41. Author conversation with members of the GUR wing of the Legion, October 2022.
42. Landoni, 'Benjamin Giorgio Galli morto a 27 anni in Ucraina: chi è il foreign fighter. La madre: "Si sentiva nel posto giusto"' ['Benjamin Giorgio Galli Died at 27 in Ukraine: Who is the Foreign Fighter. Mother: "He Felt in the Right Place"'].
43. Myroniuk and Khrebet, 'International Legion Soldiers Allege Light Weapons Misappropriation, Abuse by Commanders'. See also, Landoni, 'Benjamin Giorgio Galli morto a 27 anni in Ucraina: chi è il foreign fighter. La madre: "Si sentiva nel posto giusto"' ['Benjamin Giorgio Galli Died at 27 in Ukraine: Who is the Foreign Fighter. Mother: "He Felt in the Right Place"'].
44. Author conversation with members of the GUR wing of the Legion, November 2022.
45. Instagram account of the International Legion, @internationallegionua, post 'Today one of our teams returned from a mission and they brought a "guest"', 4 November 2022, accessed 13 April 2023.
46. Author conversation with members of the GUR wing of the Legion, November 2022.
47. See Instagram account of the GUR wing of the Legion, @international_legion_diu, more than 32,000 followers as of April 2023, accessed 13 April 2023.
48. See the two Facebook accounts: <https://www.facebook.com/InternationalLegionOfTerritorialDefenseOfUkraine>, accessed 13 April 2023 and <https://www.facebook.com/ukr.international.legion>, accessed 13 April 2023.
49. See Instagram account of the Black Team, <https://instagram.com/therealblackteam?igshid=NTc4MTIwNjQ2YQ==>, 5,300 followers as of April 2023, accessed 13 April 2023.
50. See several pictures and videos from the Instagram account of the Black Team, <https://instagram.com/therealblackteam?igshid=NTc4MTIwNjQ2YQ==>, showing naval operations as well as fighting in Bakhmut.
51. Author conversation with a former member of the GUR wing of the Legion, Ukraine, July 2022.
52. Author conversation with a former Legion platoon leader, Ukraine, July 2022.

the International Legion.[53] Volunteers are required to provide original documents showing their previous combat experience and military status. The Legion does not disclose data on the numbers of each nationality among actual recruits, but it was confirmed that the most numerous legionnaires are Americans, followed by Britons, Canadians (many of Ukrainian descent) and Poles.[54] Magrou stated in a press conference that the Legion has both fighters from Taiwan and China, although the current policy tends to exclude, with some exceptions, applicants from Russian-friendly countries, such as North Korea, Egypt and, indeed, China, that could infiltrate using spies.[55] Taiwanese volunteers are likely motivated by the analogy they see between Russia and the threat posed to their island by China.[56]

In terms of personal background, the members of the International Legion include a wide variety of professions and social profiles. Most of them are ordinary people without any previous connection to Ukraine – except ancestry in some cases – no political commitment or ideological links. As other studies clearly pointed out, unlike the 2014 flow of foreign fighters to Donbas, in 2022 the vast majority of volunteers had nothing to do with the far-right milieu.[57]

Nonetheless, some significant exceptions show mismanagement in the vetting process carried out by the Legion's staff. On 10 August 2022 the prosecutor's office in Genova, Italy, announced the opening of an investigation of 19-year-old Kevin Chiappalone,[58] who travelled to Ukraine at the end of April and joined the International Legion in early May.[59] He was an activist of the Italian neo-fascist organisation CasaPound, taking part in political rallies and showing support on his social media profiles.[60] All this content was visible and public at the time of his enlistment in the Legion. He allegedly reached Ukraine alone, without any recruitment network from Italy, flying from Milan to Krakow and then crossing the border.[61] On 23 March 2022, Kevin Chiappalone gave an anonymous interview to the Italian magazine *Panorama* saying that he is a 'far-right extremist' and that when Vladimir Putin 'pledged to de-nazify Ukraine, we felt called into question'.[62]

> The members of the International Legion include a wide variety of professions and social profiles

Already in mid-March, the Legion's spokesperson was categorical: 'We are not taking people with zero

53. Official Website of the President of Ukraine, 'Website was Launched for Foreigners Who Want to Help Ukraine Protect its Freedom and Territorial Integrity', 5 March 2022, <https://.president.gov.ua/en/news/zapuskayetsya-sajt-dlya-inozemciv-yaki-hochut-dopomogti-ukra-73361>, accessed 13 April 2023.
54. Damien Magrou, 'International Fighters Joining Ukrainian Foreign Legion', interview by Daniele Hamamdjian, *CTV News*, 15 March 2022, video (at 12:36), <https://www.youtube.com/watch?v=mLgRTrB6ets&ab_channel=CTVNews>, accessed 13 April 2023.
55. Author conversation with a former legionnaire, Ukraine, July 2022.
56. Sophie Williams, 'Why Taiwanese are Among Ukraine's Foreign Fighters', *BBC*, 13 December 2022.
57. Kacper Rekawek, 'A Trickle, Not a Flood: The Limited 2022 Far-Right Foreign Fighter Mobilization to Ukraine', *CTC Sentinel* (Vol. 15, No. 6, June 2022), <https://ctc.westpoint.edu/a-trickle-not-a-flood-the-limited-2022-far-right-foreign-fighter-mobilization-to-ukraine/>, accessed 13 April 2023.
58. *ANSA*, 'Primo italiano indagato per arruolamento con Ucraina' ['First Italian Investigated for Enlisting in Ukraine'], 11 August 2022, <https://www.ansa.it/liguria/notizie/2022/08/10/primo-italiano-indagato-per-arruolamento-con-ucraina_2e48e8ae-2280-4089-9f15-a224ad097b63.html>, accessed 13 April 2023.
59. See Facebook post, 6 May 2022, <https://www.facebook.com/InternationalLegionOfTerritorialDefenseOfUkraine/posts/pfbid0fKZCTjguif9WE2u4i1Cm7y4CsmnZmqVzgfunzbdZ8f1SA3DjkmWcvqudpahcVmswl>, accessed 13 April 2023.
60. See Facebook account, <https://www.facebook.com/kevin.chiappalone.14>, where he 'liked' pages such as the local section of CasaPound 'La Risoluta - Genova Non Conforme', CasaPound's hiking club 'La Muvra', 'Acca Larentia per non dimenticare' and 'Arditi muay thai Genova'. On his second Facebook account, under the pseudonym of 'Milza Zena', he posted a photo from a CasaPound rally held in Genova in May 2022, later removed but archived by the author, <https://www.facebook.com/milza.zena/photos>, accessed 13 April 2023.
61. *ANSA*, 'Fighter italiano, "In Ucraina non per soldi. Italia ipocrita"' ['Italian Fighter, "Not for Money in Ukraine. Hypocritical Italy"'], 12 August 2022, <https://www.ansa.it/liguria/notizie/2022/08/11/fighter-italianoin-ucraina-non-per-soldi.-italia-ipocrita_5e7f53e1-a35d-46c8-93db-4de69b09c637.html>, accessed 13 April 2023.
62. Simone Di Meo, 'o da Genova all'Ucraina per combattere Putin' ['From Genova to Ukraine to Fight Putin'], *Panorama*, 23 March 2022, <https://www.panorama.it/abbonati/Inchieste/donbass-italiano-volontario-genova>, accessed 13 April 2023.

military training [...] we need experienced, seasoned fighters'.[63] Despite halting the recruitment of applicants without combat experience in April, and the official policy of rejecting all far-right militants, Chiappalone was admitted into the Legion. In terms of military skills, he was described by a former fellow legionnaire as 'a total zero'.[64] When the investigation surfaced, the author asked both Magrou and Fuchs to confirm whether Kevin Chiappalone had actually joined the International Legion, but they never replied.[65] However, other sources confirmed that Chiappalone was indeed fighting for the International Legion, serving in the 2nd platoon of the Charlie Company in the Kharkiv sector.[66]

> Some significant exceptions show mismanagement in the vetting process carried out by the Legion's staff

This case raises questions regarding the vetting process to keep out far-right militants. In August 2022, it was reported that at least 10 Boogaloo Bois (who took part in the US Capitol insurrection) were able to join the Ukrainian forces, notably the Georgian Legion and then the 79th Air Assault Brigade, which in May suffered heavy casualties in the battle of Lyman.[67] Interestingly, the leader of CasaPound Gianluca Iannone travelled to Ukraine but did not meet Kevin Chiappalone, he instead forged a strong connection with the far-right nationalist battalion 'Revansh', which released a photo celebrating the 100th anniversary of the fascist March on Rome in 1922.[68] In February 2023, the *New York Times* reported that the Free Russia Legion, which operates under the umbrella of GUR, included a former member of the Russian Imperial Movement, who goes by the nom de guerre 'Caesar'.[69]

The Ideological Spectrum and Personal Motivations

The Political Background

In spite of the specific cases outlined, whereas in 2014–15 most of the foreign fighters joining Ukraine's ranks had a strong extremist political commitment that has functioned as a mobilisation mechanism,[70] for the 2022 wave this does not seem to be the case. Of the total number of recruits from abroad, only a very limited group comes from an extremist background.[71] A qualitative analysis of several cases shows that legionnaires cover a wide spectrum of political nuances.

In June, the International Legion posted on Facebook a short account of a volunteer's experience, describing themself as a 'lefty activist' and stating their gender identity with the preferred 'pronouns they/them'.[72] That highlights a special attention among some volunteers about gender issues and certain values, usually disapproved of by far-right groups. This is in line with opinions expressed by other legionnaires, for instance two Americans who complained about the US Supreme Court verdict that overturned Roe v. Wade, referring to the limitations to the abortion right, and said the

63. Magrou, 'International Fighters Joining Ukrainian Foreign Legion'.
64. Author conversation with a former legionnaire who enlisted and served together with Chiappalone, August 2022.
65. Author message exchange via WhatsApp and Signal with the Legion support staff, August 2022.
66. Author conversation with a former legionnaire who enlisted and served together with Chiappalone, August 2022.
67. Tess Owen and Ben Makuch, 'More Boogaloo Bois Are Heading to Ukraine to Fight', *Vice News*, 16 August 2022, <https://www.vice.com/amp/en/article/epzv8a/boogaloo-bois-ukraine-mike-dunn>, accessed 13 April 2023.
68. Photo published on Revansh Battalion's Telegram channels, 27 October 2022, showing a group of masked fighters displaying the slogan: 'La Marcia Continua' ['The March Goes On'], <https://www.instagram.com/p/CkSyXPkgCap/?igshid=YmMyMTA2M2Y%3D>, author archive.
69. Michael Schwirtz, 'They Are Russians Fighting Against Their Homeland. Here's Why', *New York Times*, 12 February 2023.
70. Emmanuel Karagiannis, 'Ukrainian Volunteer Fighters in the Eastern Front: Ideas, Political-social Norms and Emotions as Mobilization Mechanisms', *Southeast European and Black Sea Studies* (Vol. 16, No. 1, 2016), pp. 136–53.
71. Kacper Rekawek et al., 'Western Extremists and the Russian Invasion of Ukraine in 2022', Counter Extremism Project, 2022, <https://www.counterextremism.com/sites/default/files/2022-05/Western%20Extremists%20and%20the%20Russian%20Invasion%20of%20Ukraine%20in%202022_May%202022.pdf>, accessed 13 April 2023.
72. International Legion's official Facebook page, post, 21 June 2022, <https://www.facebook.com/ukr.international.legion/posts/pfbid0NzUqZNx8pdXgkVF1VeJQFheW9ecKpcGbN9RNXSdKV1Xji5h8JqQNzNJnjzAP3K6Ql>, accessed 13 April 2023.

'Taliban' were taking over the US.[73] These volunteers, from Florida and Washington state, held progressive and liberal views, and one was an atheist.

Another ideological stream involves far-left militants and anarchists, who often are more politicised and have previous combat experience in the ranks of Kurdish militias against the Islamic State. Since March, several Syria veterans have joined the Ukrainian military. Swedish volunteer Jesper Söder, who fought for the YPG (Yekîneyên Parastina Gel [People's Defence Units]) in 2015,[74] was at the Yavoriv base during the Russian strike.[75] British veteran John Harding had joined the Kurds in Syria as well, and in spring 2022 was captured by Russian troops in Mariupol while fighting alongside the Georgian Legion.[76] A fellow British volunteer, Aiden Aslin, had participated in the 2015–16 YPG offensive against Islamic State, while in 2022 he enlisted with the Ukrainian 36th Naval Infantry Brigade deployed to Mariupol, where he was also captured.[77] In September, 10 foreign volunteers, including Aiden Aslin, were released as part of a Russia–Ukraine prisoner swap mediated by Saudi Arabia.[78] In February 2023, Kremlin-backed RT released an interview with former American volunteer John McIntyre, who defected to Russia after fighting for one year in the Legion and the Karpatska Sich battalion.[79] McIntyre joined the Ukrainian ranks in March 2022 and fought in the Kharkiv sector. He told RT that his mission was to infiltrate Ukrainian units to obtain information and expose their far-right ideology because he is a communist and an anti-fascist. McIntyre claims that when he said he was in Ukraine to fight Russian imperialism and Nazis a 'guy from Croatia or Czech' answered 'the Russians aren't the Nazis, we are the Nazis'. Other foreign volunteers strongly questioned his account and described him as a lunatic and an intoxicated recruit.[80]

Anti-communist sentiment is very common among Latin American volunteers. Most of the legionnaires coming from Colombia, Argentina, Brazil, Uruguay and the Venezuelan diaspora are motivated by the idea that Russia represents the legacy of the Soviet Union.[81] They see an analogy with the socialist, authoritarian regimes of Cuba and Venezuela, but also the leftist agenda in other countries. A former member of Venezuela's Presidential Guard of Honour became disillusioned after witnessing corruption and illicit trafficking run by the Maduro regime at the notorious runway 4 (*Rampa 4*) of the Simón Bolívar International Airport of Maiquetía, Caracas. He later decided to move to Colombia and then seek asylum in France, before travelling to Ukraine.[82] In January 2023, he shared on his WhatsApp stories a video featuring late dictator Augusto Pinochet, titled 'My favourite speech of general Pinochet', in which the former Chilean strongman declares 'I'm fighting against the communists'.[83] Most Latin American volunteers appear, therefore, to hold a conservative background and a strong anti-communist motivation, including many supporters of former Brazilian president Jair Bolsonaro.[84]

Categories of Volunteers and Personal Motivations

In 2020, Kacper Rekawek identified at least three categories of foreign fighters in Ukraine: the 'resetters' who seek a new life; the 'ghosts' that come back and forth to the war zone; and the 'adventurers'

73. Author conversation with former legionnaires, Ukraine, July 2022.
74. Akbar Shahid Ahmed, 'European Fighter Just Back From Front Lines Against ISIS Says West Should Stay Vigilant', *Huffpost*, 20 November 2015.
75. Valerie Hopkins and Yousur Al-Hlou, 'Booms, Smoke and Fire Signal Horror of Russian Attack on Base', *New York Times*, 13 March 2022.
76. Sarah Haque, 'British Man in Ukraine Believed Held by Russians Appeals to Boris Johnson', *The Guardian*, 17 July 2022.
77. James Kilner, 'Captured Briton Aiden Aslin Seen Moments Before Surrender Without Head Injury Visible on Russian TV', *Daily Telegraph*, 15 April 2022.
78. Carly Olson and Dan Bilefsky, '10 Imprisoned Foreign Fighters, Including Americans, are Released as Part of a Russia-Ukraine Exchange, Saudi Arabia Says', *New York Times*, 21 September 2022.
79. Ellie Cook, 'Who is John McIntyre? American Fighting in Ukraine Defects to Russia', *Newsweek*, 1 March 2023.
80. Twitter thread, @krus_chiki, 2 March 2023, <https://twitter.com/krus_chiki/status/1631110259686219776>, accessed 13 April 2023; author conversation with a Venezuelan volunteer who served in the Legion and the Karpatska Sich battalion, February 2023.
81. Author conversation with Latin American legionnaires and volunteers, August–September 2022.
82. Author conversation with a Venezuelan former legionnaire, August–September 2022.
83. WhatsApp 'story' of the Venezuelan volunteer, 31 January 2023, author archive.
84. Instagram accounts of several Brazilian volunteers in Ukraine, author archive.

in search of adrenaline.[85] Some of these features may coincide with those applicable to the current wave of fighters, who cannot be dismissed just as far-right militants; other research described similar profiles with different nuances and goals.[86]

Several push and pull factors played a role in the decision to join the International Legion, as a qualitative analysis of volunteers' accounts show. Among the push factors, there are certainly the defence of Ukraine's sovereignty and freedom, a sense of European patriotism and solidarity, the threat perception in Poland and the Baltic countries, but also unemployment and other social issues. Pull factors include personal goals and motivations, in pursuit of realisation and a sense of belonging among peers, a desire for adventure, a quest for glory or a sort of 'combat addiction', as well as an ideological radicalisation, money or personal feelings.

Several push and pull factors played a role in the decision to join the International Legion

It is often complex to place the volunteers' profile under one single category, due to multiple overlapping and cross-cutting motivations. Among these categories, it is possible to identify 'glory seekers', 'naïve idealists' and freedom fighters, 'war tourists', some 'misfits' and renegades, the 'war addicted' veterans, as well as radicalised political activists and 'soldiers of fortune'.

Some legionnaires sincerely believe they can help Ukraine to defend its independence and freedom by taking up arms and joining the ranks of the military. This category is particularly common among American volunteers, but also Canadians and Britons. One American fighter said: 'We are here essentially to defend democracy and a nation of 44 million people which its neighbour wants to enslave'.[87] Humanitarian reasons and solidarity are recurring elements for joining the cause, as a British volunteer clarified: 'My motivation to be here, as I have a child myself, so if we were in the same situation over in the UK, I would pray for another country to come and help. The Russian army approach is inhumane'.[88]

The fulfilment of a solemn duty is shared by many volunteers, as one asserted: 'We feel privileged to be here, this is the most important place in the world right now'. Another legionnaire from the US who was asked in a press conference about his motivation to enlist, answered that when he was a young boy he had read about the horror of the Holocaust and wanted to think that if horrible evil things were happening again, he would be brave enough to do something about it.[89] This reference to the horror of the Shoah once again proves wrong the speculations about a widespread neo-Nazi or far-right influence among foreign volunteers. Interestingly, during the press conference, the local interpreter erroneously translated 'Holocaust' into Ukrainian with the word 'Holodomor', the famine provoked by Stalin's Soviet Union in Ukraine between 1932 and 1933.

A few legionnaires hold a strong religious and almost apocalyptic view of the war – even believing in miracles, such as salvos of Russian rockets missing their targets, which otherwise would have resulted in heavy losses for the Ukrainian side.[90] This special feeling also translates into a spirit of camaraderie, as Walt from Belgium said, he will remember the brotherly bond among volunteers.[91] An American

85. Kacper Rekawek, 'Career Break or a New Career? Extremist Foreign Fighters in Ukraine', report, Counter-Extremism Project, April 2020, <https://www.counterextremism.com/sites/default/files/CEP%20Report_Career%20Break%20or%20a%20New%20Career_Extremist%20Foreign%20Fighters%20in%20Ukraine_April%202020.pdf>, accessed 13 April 2023.

86. Egle E Muraskaite, 'Foreign Fighters in Ukraine: Assessing Potential Risks', Vilnius Institute for Policy Analysis, 2020, <https://vilniusinstitute.lt/wp-content/uploads/2020/02/FOREIGN-FIGHTERS-IN-UKRAINE-ASSESSING-POTENTIAL-RISKS.pdf>, accessed 13 April 2023.

87. *Radio Free Europe/Radio Liberty*, 'Ukraine's Foreign Legion: Soldiers Speak Of Historic Fight For Democracy', 27 June 2022, <https://www.youtube.com/watch?v=OnkhMBDdECc&ab_channel=RadioFreeEurope%2FRadioLiberty>, accessed 13 April 2023.

88. YouTube video, 'Legionnaires. Who's Coming to Fight for Ukraine?', *#Babylon'13*, 15 March 2022, <https://www.youtube.com/watch?v=ZBn1KYbaOms&ab_channel=%23BABYLON%2713>, accessed 13 April 2023.

89. Facebook page Kharkiv Media Hub, video 'Preszakhid Mizhnarodnoho lehionu oborony Ukrayiny' ['Press conference of the International Defense Legion of Ukraine'], Legion press conference, 8 July 2022, <https://www.facebook.com/kharkivmediahub/videos/3906939919530484>, accessed 13 April 2023.

90. Author interview with a Legion staffer, Ukraine, July 2022.

91. International Legion's official Facebook page, video 'Press Briefing Today in Kharkhiv with Three Legionnaires', 24 June 2022, <https://www.facebook.com/ukr.international.legion/posts/pfbid0cFDih8bx5tuPvFGpBut2QvZmXZGPEufT9Hqzqg5N824xNSCFWbB4ytX9Lnc8PRJ8l>, accessed 13 April 2023.

fighter confirmed this bond forged in battle and dramatic moments: 'I have the blood of my comrade on my boots and he would be alive if we had better communication equipment'.[92] Some members of the Legion seem to perceive the war uniquely as a struggle between the international volunteers and the Russian invaders.[93] Before being discharged, a legionnaire from the US donated his personal equipment worth approximately $10,000 to his comrades on the frontline, because 'what counts is my brothers'.[94]

Other profiles match both the categories of the 'glory seeker' and the 'war tourist'. For instance, a Colombian volunteer told the press: 'Why am I taking this risk? I often ask myself that and don't have an answer, I think it's also the excitement, the adrenaline, it's a chance to prove myself'.[95] Italian volunteer and Air Force cadet Giulia Schiff, who fought with the GUR wing of the Legion, said she found a personal purpose in Ukraine.[96] Former British Royal Regiment of Fusiliers sniper Christopher Perryman, serving in the 131st Separate Reconnaissance Battalion of the Ukrainian army, expressed a similar motivation on Twitter: 'I keep being asked why I came to fight someone else's war. The reason is simple! I'm not very good at anything else'.[97]

Adrien Dugay-Leyoudec, 20, and his brother Charles, 19, travelled to Ukraine without informing their parents in France.[98] This is a recurring element among younger recruits from Europe. Steven, a 19-year-old volunteer from Glasgow, did not tell his family he was heading to the warzone.[99] The same goes for two Italian young legionnaires, Benjamin Giorgio Galli and Kevin Chiappalone, who informed their parents only when they had already reached Kyiv.

Besides personal glory and 'combat addiction', some of the war veterans, especially from the US, seem to be looking for redemption from their previous experience. As a matter of fact, an American legionnaire and Iraq veteran argued that 'there's a lot of grey in the Iraq war, it's not clear right and wrong. This [Ukraine] is black and white, right versus wrong'.[100] Another former US Army soldier – although without combat experience – told the author that 'for many American veterans coming here [to Ukraine] is a sort of cleansing of their souls from previous wars in Iraq and Afghanistan'.[101]

Interestingly, this American legionnaire had Ukrainian ancestry, but decided to travel outside the US for the first time in his life to join the International Legion; likewise for a Colombian volunteer, who never left his home country before beginning his journey to war-torn Ukraine.[102] The phenomenon of the Ukrainian diaspora is mostly limited to North America and, as Naman Habtom argues, the majority of the foreign fighters are predominantly non-diasporic and lack any ethnic connection with Ukraine.[103]

Despite the lack of ethnic connection, some of the foreign volunteers began relationships with locals or dual nationals. The spokesperson for the Legion, Damien Magrou, lived in Kyiv for a few years working as an entrepreneur and in September 2022 publicly announced quitting his position to –

92. Author conversation with a former legionnaire, Ukraine, July 2022.
93. Author interview with a Legion staffer, Ukraine, July 2022; author conversation with a German analyst in Ukraine, July 2022.
94. Author conversation with a former legionnaire, Ukraine, July 2022.
95. YouTube video, 'Foreigners Fighting for Ukraine', *DW Documentary*, 9 May 2022, <https://www.youtube.com/watch?v=csyGP2taOtE&ab_channel=DWDocumentary>, accessed 13 April 2023.
96. *AGI*, 'È facile dirsi pacifisti se si vive in Italia e non si combatte in Ucraina' '[It's Easy to Call Oneself a Pacifist if You Live in Italy and Not Fighting in Ukraine'], 16 October 2022, <https://www.agi.it/cronaca/news/2022-10-16/ucraina-giulia-schiff-italiani-vogliono-pace-non-vivono-guerra-18467631/>, accessed 13 April 2023.
97. Christopher Perryman's Twitter account, @pezz57, 3 February 2023, <https://twitter.com/pezz57/status/1621516301670948864>, accessed 13 April 2023.
98. Faustine Vincent, 'Adrien Dugay-Leyoudec, deuxième combattant français tué en Ukraine, parti défendre une « cause juste »' ['Adrien Dugay-Leyoudec Second French Fighter Killed in Ukraine, Set Off to Defend a "Just Cause"'], *Le Monde*, 9 July 2022.
99. YouTube video, 'Legionnaires. Who's Coming to Fight for Ukraine?', *#Babylon'13*, 15 March 2022, <https://www.youtube.com/watch?v=ZBn1KYbaOms&ab_channel=%23BABYLON%2713>, accessed 13 April 2023.
100. *Radio Free Europe/Radio Liberty*, 'Ukraine's Foreign Legion: Soldiers Speak of Historic Fight For Democracy'.
101. Author conversation with a legionnaire, Ukraine, July 2022.
102. YouTube, 'Foreigners Fighting for Ukraine', *DW Documentary*.
103. Naman Karl-Thomas Habtom, 'The Composition and Challenges of Foreign Fighters in Ukraine', *Scandinavian Journal of Military Studies* (Vol. 5, No. 1, 2022), pp. 79–90.

among other reasons – focus on the marriage with his girlfriend from Sumy.[104] Former Italian Air Force cadet Giulia Jasmine Schiff started a relationship with an Israel Defense Forces tank commander known in Ukraine as 'Mr. Wolf' with the rank of captain,[105] and joined his Israeli-Ukrainian unit 'Masada' to fight together,[106] having herself Jewish-Egyptian origins.[107] Masada later merged into the Stugna Battalion. In spite of the Russian propaganda narrative about the neo-Nazi identity among foreign volunteers, Giulia Schiff was not the only Jewish fighter. Italian volunteer Benjamin Giorgio Galli, who died in September, had Jewish ancestry as well and was given a Jewish funeral in Kyiv.[108]

A small portion of foreigners were motivated by pecuniary and economic gain as well. A Colombian volunteer who fought for the GUR wing of the Legion, for instance, took his decision based on the remuneration, among other things. As a former Colombian Army special forces soldier, he was contracted by the United Arab Emirates' military to fight in Yemen against the Houthi insurgency,[109] just like thousands of other Latin American mercenaries do.[110] In 2021 he joined, as a gunman, the Mexican criminal syndicate *Cárteles Unidos*, also known as *La Resistencia*, at war with the *Jalisco Nueva Generación* drug cartel.[111] Following the Russian invasion, he decided to enlist with the Legion because of the significant combat benefits, but also due to the fact he was wanted in Colombia for unspecified criminal charges.

Some analysts have pointed out that several individuals with a criminal background or prior convictions may have reached Ukraine to avoid prosecution or serving a sentence in their home countries. Besides the Polish gangster Piotr 'Broda' Kapuscinski, there are other known cases of wanted volunteers, such as the previously mentioned Colombian fighter who spent time working for the *narcos*. The *New York Times* reported that Willy Joseph Cancel from Kentucky, who died in Ukraine, was discharged for bad conduct from the US Marine Corps after serving time in a military jail for an undisclosed criminal offence.[112] Finland's public broadcast service also claimed that among those who travelled to Ukraine there are members of Finnish motorcycle gangs with a criminal background.[113]

A small portion of foreigners were motivated by pecuniary and economic gain as well

As for the case of foreign fighters alongside the Kurdish militias in Syria, Western governments and counterterrorism institutions are concerned about returning foreign fighters with links to anarchist or neo-fascist movements. The combat experience acquired in Ukraine, the knowledge of military tactics, international networks and perhaps even access to weapons are deemed high-risk factors.[114] Therefore, national security agencies and EU institutions are

104. Damien Magrou's LinkedIn post, 13 September 2022, <https://www.linkedin.com/posts/damienmagrou_hi-everyone-i-have-several-announcements-activity-6975118976657805312-6tnB?utm_source=share&utm_medium=member_desktop>, accessed 13 April 2023.
105. Instagram account, "zeevfrei", author archive, 15 February 2023.
106. *Times of Israel*, 'Daily Briefing Aug. 8: As Sun Sets on Operation Breaking Dawn, Some Rays of Hope', 8 August 2022, <https://www.timesofisrael.com/daily-briefing-aug-8-as-sun-sets-on-operation-breaking-dawn-some-rays-of-hope/>, accessed 13 April 2023.
107. Instagram account of Giulia Jasmine Schiff, @giuliajschiff, story, 17 February 2023, author archive.
108. *ANSA*, 'Ucraina: a Kiev i funerali del foreign fighter italiano' ['Funeral of Italian Foreign Fighter in Kyiv'], 24 September 2022, <https://www.ansa.it/sito/notizie/cronaca/2022/09/24/ucraina-a-kiev-i-funerali-del-foreign-fighter-italiano_2c330473-aecc-4d36-835d-4b2221fc28a6.html>, accessed 13 April 2023.
109. Author conversation with a former GUR wing legionnaire, Ukraine, July 2022.
110. Andreas Krieg, 'The UAE's "Dogs of War": Boosting a Small State's Regional Power Projection', *Small Wars and Insurgencies* (Vol. 33, No. 1–2, 2022), pp. 152–72.
111. Cárteles Unidos, *Insight Crime*, latest update 18 July 2022, <https://insightcrime.org/mexico-organized-crime-news/carteles-unidos/>, accessed 13 April 2023.
112. Jane Arraf, 'Deaths of Foreign Fighters Draw Renewed Attention to the Military Volunteers in Ukraine', *New York Times*, 1 May 2022.
113. Mikko Gustafsson and Julie Ebbe, 'Undre världens män har sökt sig från Finland till kriget i Ukraina' ['Men of the Underworld from Finland Joined the War in Ukraine'], *Yle*, 25 March 2022, <https://svenska.yle.fi/a/7-10014654>, accessed 13 April 2023.
114. See, for instance, Teun van Dongen et al., 'Foreign Volunteers in Ukraine: Security Considerations for Europe', ICCT, 4 May 2022, <https://www.icct.nl/publication/foreign-volunteers-in-ukraine-security-considerations-for-europe>, accessed 13 April 2023.

closely monitoring the flow of volunteers and their personal connections.[115] This risk is combined with the proliferation of Ukrainian passports provided to the foreigners by GUR and integration in Ukrainian society, sometimes through far-right organisations such as *Pravyj Sektor* or the Azov milieu.

Conclusion

The International Legion of Defence of Ukraine represents a small portion of thousands of foreign volunteers, many of whom spent only a few weeks or months at the frontline before heading back home. This high turnover prevented the creation of a cohesive and consolidated unit, with many skilled fighters opting for other military formations. The Legion managed to deploy an infantry battalion, while other volunteers were detached to Territorial Defence and Ground Forces brigades. Ukraine's military intelligence (GUR) absorbed the war veterans in newly established units, such as the 3rd Battalion. In the first, dramatic phase of the invasion, they may have provided a significant contribution in the defence of Kyiv, fresh manpower and a morale boost, but after the flow of heavy weapons they became less relevant on a military level. The Ukrainian government may have used the Legion as a political tool to attract international solidarity and urge Western governments to do more.

The majority of legionnaires come from North America, Europe and Latin America, but are led by a diverse set of motivations, have a variety of personal backgrounds and the majority has no previous political affiliation. Most importantly, returning fighters seem not to be radicalised after their experience in Ukraine,[116] but are either grateful for the fraternal bond of camaraderie among legionnaires, or disillusioned and traumatised. Small segments hold far-right or conservative views, but others come from the anarchist milieu and fought for the Kurds in Syria against the Islamic State. Both factions were unable to radicalise new recruits, who remained focused on the defence of Ukraine. ■

Matteo Pugliese is a PhD candidate at the University of Barcelona, working on the role of prison intelligence in counterterrorism. He is also a Reserve Officer of Italian Carabinieri and served in the General Commander's Staff on international cooperation and counterterrorism issues. Between 2017 and 2022, he was an Associate Research Fellow of the Italian Institute for International Political Studies (ISPI). His publications have featured in the West Point Combating Terrorism Centre's journal *Sentinel* and the Italian domestic intelligence agency's magazine *Gnosis*.

115. Author conversations with Italian and Spanish counterterrorism officials, Rome and Madrid, June and September 2022; author conversations with a Frontex official, Warsaw, July and October 2022.
116. Kacper Rekawek, 'A Year of Foreign Fighting in Ukraine. Catching Fish with Bare Hands?', Counter Extremism Project, 16 March 2023, <https://www.counterextremism.com/press/cep-report-year-foreign-fighting-ukraine>, accessed 13 April 2023.

India's Response to the War in Ukraine

Evaluating the Balancing Act

Shubhrajeet Konwer

Shubhrajeet Konwer analyses New Delhi's position on the war in Ukraine and the limits of its delicate 'balancing act'. He argues that India's relations with the West have crossed the minimum threshold level of cooperation and as such both parties need to handle each other's misgivings. New Delhi's perspective towards Russia's invasion of Ukraine is only likely to change if there is substantial reversal of Russia's position on issues related to India's national security.

The protracted war of attrition in Ukraine is a turning point in world politics. It has not only redrawn a 'red line' in Europe, but has shaken the foundation of the neoliberal world order and challenged the established norms of non-intervention. It has reignited the debate on 'hedging' and the stance of 'neutral' nations in times of war.[1] While Washington and its core allies have reacted by placing economic sanctions on Russia, New Delhi has taken a more nuanced stance on the Ukrainian conflict and has not condemned Russia's actions.

India's government, which has always advocated for 'territorial integrity' and the 'peaceful settlement of disputes', is now the object of intense courtship from a variety of quarters, as Russia's invasion of Ukraine heightens renewed rivalry among global superpowers. However, as things stand, Narendra Modi's administration remains dedicated to safeguarding its perceived national interests by continuing to pursue a difficult balancing act.

Given its past record, India's decision to remain 'neutral' and not condemn Russia's invasion of Ukraine is not a surprise, but a well-trodden strategy of Indian foreign policy. India has been relatively soft on Russia since the end of the Cold War: New Delhi did not condemn Moscow for its involvement in the war with Georgia (2008) or its annexation of Crimea (2014).[2] In 2001, rather than abstaining, India went one step further by voting against the UN resolution condemning human rights violations in Chechnya.[3] Given Russia's record of supporting India's 'national interests' at various international forums, and its strong defence ties and challenges along the Line of Actual Control (LAC), New Delhi continues to uphold its relationship with Moscow. For New Delhi, the potential benefits of maintaining good relations with Moscow outweigh the risks. Moreover, the geopolitical fallout of Russia's invasion of Ukraine has tested India's 'natural partnership'[4] with the US-led West. Even though several international dignitaries

1. John D Ciorciari and Jürgen Haacke, 'Hedging in International Relations: An Introduction', *International Relations of the Asia-Pacific* (Vol. 19, No. 3, September 2019), pp. 367–74.
2. Petr Topychkanov, 'India the Abstainer', Carnegie Endowment for International Peace, 4 August 2014, <https://carnegiemoscow.org/commentary/55272>, accessed 25 October 2022.
3. Human Rights Watch, 'U.N. Resolution on Chechnya Welcomed', 19 April 2001, <https://www.hrw.org/news/2001/04/19/un-resolution-chechnya-welcomed>, accessed 8 July 2022.
4. Sridhar Kumaraswami, 'India, US Natural Partners: PM Modi', *Deccan Chronicle*, 12 April 2022, <https://www.deccanchronicle.com/nation/current-affairs/120422/india-us-natural-partners-pm-modi.html>, accessed 31 March 2023.

President of Russia Vladimir Putin with Prime Minister of India Narendra Modi during the 21st India – Russia Annual Summit, 2021. *Courtesy PIB / Alamy Stock Photo*

have visited India since the commencement of the war, New Delhi has maintained that it has the right to take its own position. External Affairs Minister (EAM, Government of India) Subrahmanyam Jaishankar's statement that '[India is] not sitting on the fence' and is instead 'sitting on [its] ground' encapsulates New Delhi's stance on the dispute.[5]

India's 'Nuanced' Position in the War

Three months after the 21st India – Russia Annual Summit in New Delhi (December 2021),[6] which was attended by President Vladimir Putin, Russia's invasion of Ukraine in February 2022 has put India in a tight spot. The Modi government has adopted a multifaceted strategy to deal with the fallout of the war in Ukraine. The position that India takes on Ukraine is informed by its perceived 'national interest'.[7] New Delhi's strategy includes lobbying for peace and dialogue, extracting trade benefits from Moscow, and leveraging its position to obtain benefits from the West. External Affairs Minister S Jaishankar has reiterated that 'India is on the side of peace'.[8] It is important to note that India abstained from the resolution in the UN Security Council condemning Russia's illegitimate referenda and annexation of the four regions of Ukraine.[9]

5. Geeta Mohan, 'India's Foreign Policy isn't about Sitting on Fence: S Jaishankar', *India Today*, 4 June 2022, <https://www.indiatoday.in/india/story/india-foreign-policy-sitting-on-fence-s-jaishankar-globsec-2022-1958080-2022-06-03>, accessed 25 October 2022.
6. The 21st India–Russia Annual Summit was held in New Delhi on 6 December 2021. Further details are available at Press Information Bureau, Government of India, <https://pib.gov.in/PressReleasePage.aspx?PRID=1778665>, accessed 30 March 2023.
7. *Economic Times*, '"In Our National Interest...," says Jaishankar as He Explains India-Russia Relationship', 28 September 2022, <https://economictimes.indiatimes.com/news/india/in-our-national-interest-says-jaishankar-as-he-explains-india-russia-relationship/articleshow/94493332.cms>, accessed 25 October 2022.
8. *India Today*, 'India is on the Side of Peace: Jaishankar on Russia-Ukraine War at UNGA', 25 September 2022, <https://www.indiatoday.in/india/story/india-on-side-of-peace-jaishankar-on-russia-ukraine-war-unga-2004443-2022-09-25>, accessed 25 October 2022.
9. *Business Standard*, 'India Abstains from UNSC Resolution on Russian Annexation of Ukraine's Land', 1 October 2022, <https://www.business-standard.com/article/international/india-abstains-from-unsc-resolution-on-russian-annexation-of-ukraine-s-land-122100100023_1.html>, accessed 25 October 2022.

DOI: 10.1080/03071847.2023.2220762

India's Response to the War in Ukraine

As evidenced by data collected by the IMF, the war in Ukraine has caused significant economic problems worldwide; prices have risen around the world, especially for oil and natural gas, as well as for food and wheat.[10] Many developing countries, including India, have felt the detrimental effects of the Ukraine crisis in the form of higher inflation and a halt in economic growth. To offset the negative impact of the war on its economy, New Delhi has taken a soft approach towards the conflict by continuing to purchase oil at 'discounted' rates from Russia and 'prioritizing its own energy needs'.[11] The government of India resolutely refused to condemn Russia's invasion of Ukraine and has, so far, merely 'expressed concern'.[12]

The Modi administration, conscious of the political and fiscal context in India, has taken such action as a result of the slowing economy – increased gas prices particularly have affected its constituents. The Reserve Bank of India estimates that it will take India until 2034–35 to recover economically from the losses it has sustained as a result of the Covid-19 pandemic.[13] Additionally, since India imports 80% of its oil, the war in Ukraine has impacted oil prices in India.[14] The Modi administration has opted to push for its trade ties with Moscow. As reports indicate, there has been 'unprecedented growth' in trade relations between the two countries; the trade turnover in the first half of 2022 reached over $11 billion and it is expected that mutual trade will touch $30 billion by 2025.[15] According to India's Ministry of Commerce and Industry, largely helped by the import of oil and fertilisers, bilateral trade between New Delhi and Moscow has touched a record high of $18.2 billion between April and August 2022.[16] Oil purchases from Russia were defended by External Affairs Minister Jaishankar, who stated that the increase in oil prices caused by the Russia–Ukraine war is 'breaking our back'.[17] Besides oil and gas, India has also stepped up imports from Russia in other sector. Reports suggest that between April and July 2022, India spent $276 million on sunflower oil from Russia, more than doubling its purchase price from the previous year's $129 million; in addition, a total of $60 million was spent on silver imports from Russia.[18]

Indian businesses are looking to fill the hole left by Western firms that have either declared or

10. Alfred Kammer et al., 'How War in Ukraine Is Reverberating Across World's Regions', *IMF Blog*, 15 March 2022, <https://www.imf.org/en/Blogs/Articles/2022/03/15/blog-how-war-in-ukraine-is-reverberating-across-worlds-regions-031522#:~:text=The%20conflict%20is%20a%20major,slower%20growth%20and%20faster%20inflation>, accessed 25 October 2022.
11. Sheikh Saaliq, 'India Signals it Will Continue to Buy Oil From Russia', *AP News*, 5 December 2022, <https://apnews.com/article/europe-business-india-new-delhi-global-trade-5a3c6918853047a42ac4be1d6062128a>, accessed 30 March 2023.
12. Shubhajit Roy, 'As Russia Hits Ukraine Cities, India Says "Deeply Concerned at Escalation"', *Indian Express*, 11 October 2022, <https://indianexpress.com/article/india/deeply-concerned-over-escalation-of-conflict-in-ukraine-india-8200952/>, accessed 30 March 2023.
13. Siddhartha Upasani, 'Indian Economy to Overcome COVID Losses Only in FY35, says RBI Report', *Money Control*, 29 April 2022, <https://www.moneycontrol.com/news/business/economy/indian-economy-to-overcome-covid-losses-only-in-fy35-says-rbi-report-8431811.html>, accessed 25 October 2022.
14. *Economic Times*, 'Oil Prices Up Due to Russia-Ukraine War: Gadkari', 26 March 2022, <https://m.economictimes.com/industry/energy/oil-gas/oil-prices-up-due-to-russia-ukraine-war-gadkari/articleshow/90452821.cms>, accessed 30 March 2023.
15. *Economic Times*, 'Russia-India Trade Turnover Witnesses "Unprecedented Growth" in First Half of 2022: Russian Envoy', 14 September 2022, <https://economictimes.indiatimes.com/news/economy/foreign-trade/russia-india-trade-turnover-witnesses-unprecedented-growth-in-first-half-of-2022-russian-envoy/articleshow/94207178.cms?utm_source=contentofinterest&utm_medium=text&utm_campaign=cppst>, accessed 25 October 2022.
16. Harikishan Sharma, 'India-Russia Trade Soars to Record High as Imports of Oil and Fertiliser Drive Surge', *Indian Express*, 21 October 2022, <https://indianexpress.com/article/india/india-russia-trade-soars-to-record-high-as-imports-of-oil-and-fertiliser-drive-surge-8221831/>, accessed 25 October 2022.
17. *Financial Express*, 'Spike in Oil Price Due to Russia-Ukraine Conflict Breaking India's Back: S Jaishankar', 28 September 2022, <https://www.financialexpress.com/defence/spike-in-oil-price-breaking-indias-back-jaishankar/2693938/> accessed 25 October 2022.
18. Dilasha Seth and Ravi Dutta Mishra, 'Non-oil Imports from Russia Surge; Exports Face Hurdles', *Mint*, 24 September 2022, <https://www.livemint.com/news/world/nonoil-imports-from-russia-surge-exports-face-hurdles-11663954508418.html>, accessed 25 October 2022.

completed their withdrawal from the Russian market in the aftermath of recent economic sanctions.[19] It is worth repeating that Moscow and New Delhi are in talks to establish a bilateral agreement under which the ruble and the rupee may be used in bilateral transactions. Reports indicate that Moscow and New Delhi have been discussing the possibility of mutually accepting each other's payment cards, such as Russia's Mir and India's RuPay, as well as alternative methods for implementing each other's interbank transfer systems, such as India's Unified Payments Interface (UPI) and SPFS;[20] according to reports, an Indian business has also bought coal from Russia and paid for it in yuan.[21] The State Bank of India, India's largest bank, is also working on a framework to facilitate foreign trade and business using the Indian rupee.[22] At a time when Europe and the US are facing their worst security crises, India's commitment to pursue its national interests steadfastly has not been well received in the West.

New Delhi's view on the conflict is also related to its defence connections with Moscow as much of India's defence equipment is of Soviet origin. According to reports, between 2000 and 2020, Russia accounted for 66.5 % of India's arms imports.[23] Besides, there are a number of different bilateral projects that are currently being worked on. Some of these projects include the 'licensed manufacturing of T-90 tanks and Su-30-MKI aircraft, the delivery of MiG-29-K aircraft and Kamov-31, and the upgrading of MiG-29 aircraft'.[24] In addition, joint military exercises (INDRA) and cooperation in the production of military platforms (BrahMos cruise missiles) have also been the hallmark of the Russia–India relationship. Therefore, in spite of a decline in arms imports from Russia, it still stood at 46% in 2017–21.[25]

While there was a brief lull in diplomatic relations between Moscow and New Delhi, the departure of US forces from Afghanistan in August 2021 provided the climate and momentum for Russia to strengthen its presence in Afghanistan and bolster its ties with India. It must be recalled that for New Delhi, issues of peace, stability and democracy in Afghanistan are of prime concern. The return of the Taliban to Afghanistan not only throttles the democratic space but also threatens the groundwork for peace in India's Jammu and Kashmir. [26] In December 2021, Vladimir Putin travelled to India to bridge the gap that was then opening up between Moscow and New Delhi, particularly on matters related to India's growing participation in the Quad and its differences with China.[27] The 2+2 Ministerial Dialogue, which took place on the margins of this summit, further boosted the 'special and privileged strategic partnership'.[28] The two nations resolved to extend their accord

19. Rasul Bailay, 'As Global Brands Take Flight, Indian Retailers Book Tickets for Russia', *Economic Times*, 12 April 2022, <https://economictimes.indiatimes.com/industry/services/retail/as-global-brands-take-flight-indian-retailers-book-tickets-for-russia/articleshow/90788758.cms?from=mdr>, accessed 25 October 2022.
20. *Russia Briefing*, 'Russia-India Trade Up 120% In 2022', 14 September 2022, <https://www.russia-briefing.com/news/russia-india-trade-up-120-in-2022.html/>, accessed 25 October 2022.
21. Sudarshan Varadhan, Nupur Anand and Aftab Ahmed, 'How an Indian Cement Maker Bought Russian Coal using Yuan', *Reuters*, 8 July 2022, <https://www.reuters.com/markets/commodities/exclusive-how-an-indian-cement-maker-bought-russian-coal-using-yuan-2022-07-07/>, accessed 1 April 2023.
22. *Deccan Herald*, 'India has Decided to Authorise SBI to Promote Rupee Trade with Russia: FIEO President', 14 September 2022, <https://www.deccanherald.com/national/india-has-decided-to-authorise-sbi-to-promote-rupee-trade-with-russia-fieo-president-1145101.html>, accessed 25 October 2022.
23. Krishn Kaushik, 'Explained: How Dependent is India on Russia's Weapons?', *Indian Express*, 3 March 2022, <https://indianexpress.com/article/explained/india-russia-military-weapons-defence-ties-7795804/>, accessed 30 March 2023.
24. Embassy of India in Moscow, 'India Russia Defence Cooperation', 2022, <https://indianembassy-moscow.gov.in/india-russia-defence-cooperation.php#:~:text=It%20is%20guided%20by%20the,entry%20into%20force%20is%20underway>, accessed 25 October 2022.
25. *Economic Times*, 'Russia's Share of Arms Import to India Fell from 69% in 2012-17 to 46% in 2017-21: Report', 15 March 2022, <https://economictimes.indiatimes.com/news/defence/russias-share-of-arms-import-to-india-fell-from-69-in-2012-17-to-46-in-2017-21-report/articleshow/90218483.cms>, accessed 13 July 2022.
26. Ayjaz Wani, 'Resurgent Taliban and its Implications on Kashmir', *Observer Research Foundation*, 30 August 2021, <https://www.orfonline.org/expert-speak/resurgent-taliban-and-its-implications-on-kashmir/>, accessed 30 March 2023.
27. Rajeswari Pillai Rajagopalan, 'Why Did Russian President Putin Visit India?', *Observer Research Foundation*, 15 December 2021, <https://www.orfonline.org/research/why-did-russian-president-putin-visit-india/>, accessed 30 March 2023.
28. During the visit of President Dmitry Medvedev to India in December 2010, it was decided to further elevate the India-Russia strategic partnership to the level of a 'special and privileged strategic partnership'.

of military and technological cooperation until 2031 during Putin's visit.[29] For New Delhi, Russia's presence and diplomatic backing are critical if it is to achieve two crucial strategic challenges: first, preventing Afghanistan from becoming a 'safe haven for global terror organisations';[30] and second, 'managing China in the short term'.[31] New Delhi needs healthy ties with Moscow to counter Beijing's looming presence along the LAC. According to Grossman, 'India further seeks to leverage strong ties with Russia against its Chinese adversary, and greatly appreciates Moscow's support of its position on disputed Kashmir'.[32] Given India's strategic challenges in South Asia and the compulsions of its domestic economy, the Modi government has little choice but to embrace Moscow as a counterbalance to both China and the US.

Ramifications for New Delhi

The fallout of India's 'neutral' stand will have immediate as well as long-term implications for New Delhi. In the short term, by conducting a significant amount of business with Moscow, New Delhi has been able to temporarily mitigate some of the adverse effects of the nation's ongoing economic challenges. Like the rest of the developing world, reports suggest that India, along with several others, had a 'net positive view of Russia';[33] domestic audiences continue to back the Modi administration.[34] Furthermore, according to a survey, a sizeable section of the Indian population is against Western sanctions against Russia.[35] At home, at least, the Modi administration is triumphing in the 'perception fight'. India's stance has been generally approved by both domestic security experts[36] and the general public.[37] However, New Delhi must be prepared for the long-term ramifications of its stand on the conflict. As the war continues unabated, India's lopsided defence relationship with Russia is likely to be further strained, and so too will its natural relationship with the West. The growing camaraderie between Moscow and Beijing is also a major source of concern for India.

The 'cornerstone' of Russia–India relations is defence cooperation, which would be seriously harmed by the situation in Ukraine over the long run. The war in Ukraine has entered its second year with no meaningful solution on the horizon. According to a number of sources, the Russian military has sustained significant casualties[38] and is afflicted with 'an acute shortage of people,

29. Saheli Roy Choudhury, 'India and Russia Broaden Defense Ties Despite Potential Risk of U.S. Sanctions', *CNBC*, 7 December 2021, <https://www.cnbc.com/2021/12/07/india-russia-broaden-ties-and-military-cooperation.html>, accessed 30 March 2023.
30. Devirupa Mitra, 'India-Russia Summit: Modi, Putin Decide to Provide "Immediate" Humanitarian Aid to Afghanistan', *The Wire*, 7 December 2021, <https://thewire.in/diplomacy/india-russia-summit-modi-putin-decide-to-provide-immediate-humanitarian-aid-to-afghanistan>, accessed 25 October 2022.
31. Lee Ying Shan, 'India's Military Relationship with Russia isn't Going Away – It'll "Endure for Decades", Analyst Says', *CNBC*, 28 September 2022, <https://www.cnbc.com/2022/09/29/indias-military-ties-with-russia-will-endure-for-decades-analyst.html>, accessed 1 April 2023.
32. Derek Grossman, 'Russia Looks Less and Less Like India's Friend', *RAND Blog*, 4 March 2022, <https://www.rand.org/blog/2022/03/russia-looks-less-and-less-like-indias-friend.html>, accessed 16 July 2022.
33. Patrick Wintour, 'Negative Views of Russia Mainly Limited to Western Liberal Democracies, Poll Shows', *The Guardian*, 30 May 2022.
34. *Indian Express*, 'Majority of Indians Follow Russia-Ukraine War, but Against New Delhi's Military Involvement, Says Survey', 16 May 2022, <https://indianexpress.com/article/world/russia-ukraine-war-indians-survey-7920614/>, accessed 17 July 2022.
35. Sana Ali, '6 in 10 Support Indian Govt's Handling of the Russia-Ukraine Crisis, Says Survey', *Business Today*, 3 March 2022, <https://www.businesstoday.in/latest/world/story/6-in-10-support-indian-govts-handling-of-the-russia-ukraine-crisis-says-survey-324601-2022-03-03>, accessed 16 July 2022.
36. Krishna N Das and Devjyot Ghoshal, 'Analysis: India Sharpens Stand on Ukraine War but Business as Usual with Russia', *Reuters*, 28 September 2022.
37. Sunainaa Chadha, '6 in 10 Indians Satisfied with India's Decision of not Voting on the UN Resolution against Russia: Survey', *Times of India*, 3 March 2022, <https://timesofindia.indiatimes.com/business/india-business/6-in-10-indians-satisfied-with-indias-decision-of-not-voting-on-un-resolution-against-russia-survey/articleshow/89968765.cms>, accessed 30 March 2023.
38. *Associated Press*, 'Explainer: Russia's Military Woes Mount Amid Ukraine Attacks', 6 October 2022, <https://apnews.com/article/russia-ukraine-putin-6ef2407371c67f0736459378833fab7a>, accessed 25 October 2022. See also Helene Cooper,

lack of coordination between units, and unstable supply lines'.[39] Meanwhile, although effects of the war are being felt in the Russian economy, which is expected to shrink, 'it is not hurting enough' to alter the course of the war.[40] Moscow expects 'war fatigue' to set in among Western nations; the war is definitely testing the resilience of the EU and the US financially.[41] Significantly, as the war has gotten more lethal, the chasm between Russia and the West has become almost insurmountable. Given the asymmetric defence relationship with Moscow, New Delhi is increasingly feeling uneasy.

Defence Cooperation and Trade

At the inaugural 2+2 Dialogue of the Foreign and Defence Ministers of India and the Russian Federation (December 2021, New Delhi), the two countries signed the Agreement on the Programme for Military Technical Cooperation for 2021–31.[42] It entailed several bilateral projects, joint research and design development, as well as thrust to joint ventures under the 'Make in India' initiative.[43] A year later, considering the difficulties the Russian military is having, it is plausible to infer that many cooperative projects are in jeopardy despite the lack of an official announcement on their future. Contradictory reports have since emerged, with the Russian government insisting that the delivery of the S-400 missile systems is on track and will be delivered to India by the end of the year;[44] but given the circumstances, experts conclude that 'big ticket' defence instruments like the S-400 missile systems, spares for Kilo-Class submarines, Mig-29 aircraft, and Mi-17 military transport helicopters, are likely to be delayed.[45] Another report suggests that the 'delivery of the two *Krivak-* or *Talwar-*class stealth frigates under construction for the Indian Navy in Russia' will be delayed due to the war in Ukraine.[46]. The war in Ukraine is therefore starting to have an impact on India's defence needs and 'India's dependence on Russian arms has been gradually tapering'.[47] India has embarked on a journey of diversification of its defence supply. Although India continues to be the world's biggest arms buyer, Russian arms shipments to India, the country that purchases the most Russian weapons, decreased by 37% between 2018 and 2022, according to the Stockholm International Peace Research Institute (SIPRI).[48]

Eric Schmitt and Thomas Gibbons-Neff, 'Soaring Death Toll Gives Grim Insight Into Russian Tactics', *New York Times*, 2 February 2023.

39. *Hindustan Times*, 'A Look at Russia's Losses in Ukraine Amid Annexation Boast', 6 October 2022, <https://www.hindustantimes.com/world-news/a-look-at-russia-s-losses-in-ukraine-amid-annexation-boast-101665037003550.html>, accessed 25 October 2022.
40. *Mint*, 'How is Russian Economy Doing under Western Sanctions?', 31 August 2022, <https://www.livemint.com/opinion/online-views/how-is-russian-economy-doing-under-western-sanctions-11661885439189.html>, accessed 25 October 2022.
41. Institut Montaigne, 'Interview with Ivan Kratsev: The Ukraine War: A Resilience Test for the European Union?', 15 September 2022, <https://www.institutmontaigne.org/en/expressions/ukraine-war-resilience-test-european-union>, accessed 25 October 2022.
42. Embassy of India, 'India-Russia Defence Cooperation', <https://indianembassy-moscow.gov.in/india-russia-defence-cooperation.php#:~:text=Bilateral%20Relations%3A%20India%2DRussia%20Relations&text=It%20is%20guided%20by%20the,Delhi%20on%206th%20December%202021>, accessed 30 March 2023.
43. *Ibid*.
44. Manu Pubby, 'No Delay, S-400 to Arrive by December; System "Guaranteed" to Perform at 3000m; No Covid-19 Impact on Production', *Economic Times*, 25 June 2021, <https://economictimes.indiatimes.com/news/defence/no-delay-s-400-to-arrive-by-dec/articleshow/83820346.cms?from=mdr>, accessed 25 October 2022.
45. Vivek Raghuvanshi, 'India Braces for Sanctions on Russia to Delay Weapons Programs, Deliveries', *Defense News*, 2 March 2022, <https://www.defensenews.com/global/asia-pacific/2022/03/02/india-braces-for-sanctions-on-russia-to-delay-weapons-programs-deliveries/>, accessed 25 October 2022.
46. Dinakar Peri, 'Six-month Delay in Delivery of Two Stealth Frigates by Russia Due to War in Ukraine', *The Hindu*, 17 August 2022, <https://www.thehindu.com/news/national/six-month-delay-in-delivery-of-two-stealth-frigates-by-russia-due-to-war-in-ukraine/article65779161.ece>, accessed 25 October 2022.
47. *Economist Intelligence Unit*, 'Defence Supply Diversification is on Track in India', 29 July 2022, <http://country.eiu.com/article.aspx?articleid=552319238&Country=India&topic=Economy&subtopic=Fore_3>, accessed 25 October 2022.
48. SIPRI, 'Surge in Arms Imports to Europe, While US Dominance of the Global Arms Trade Increases', 13 March 2023, <https://www.sipri.org/media/press-release/2023/surge-arms-imports-europe-while-us-dominance-global-arms-trade-increases>, accessed 1 April 2023.

According to reports, the US–India defence partnership is already gathering steam in an effort to offset China's threat and lessen reliance on Russian weapons.[49] Additionally, France continues to woo India, and its diplomats have expressed openness to working with India on major projects, including nuclear-powered submarines. France has handed India 36 Rafale fighter jets and other weaponry and is building a national-level defence industrial base.[50] India continues to strengthen its defence ties with Israel and collaborate in areas of unmanned aerial vehicles (UAV), advanced surveillance technologies, cyber defence capabilities and electronic warfare systems.[51]

Security experts have highlighted that the Indian government has taken a number of regulatory measures to encourage the design, development and domestic production of defence equipment, with the ultimate goal of creating a 'sustainable defence industrial ecosystem'.[52] India is seeking to diversify its defence procurement and is propagating 'buy and make (Indian)'.[53] The push for 'atmanirbhar' (self-reliance) in defence production has also gathered steam, especially after the skirmishes with China in Galwan Valley in May 2020, where India 'scrambled across the globe to purchase military hardware'.[54] The Modi administration is determined to avoid the errors of the past. It is expected that the creation of seven new defence Public Sector Undertakings (PSUs) in October 2021, which are completely government owned entities, 'will help in improving the country's self-reliance in defence preparedness'.[55] The government's push for indigenisation of 'firepower', which includes production of Light Combat Aircraft (LCA), Light Utility Helicopter (LUH), operationalisation of the Dhanush gun system along the borders of China (Ladakh sector) and modernisation under the army's Field Artillery Rationalisation Plan (FARP), are some of the major steps towards making India's military less dependent on other parties.[56] Defence Minister Rajnath Singh has said that lessons may be learned from the crisis in Ukraine, and that these lessons apply not just to logistics but also to economic relations and commercial contracts, which may be disrupted during future wars.[57] Therefore, the government of India intends to buy a number of unmanned aerial platforms during the next several years to carry out surveillance operations in the LAC. The Hindustan Aeronautics Ltd is already working hard on 'AI-driven multi-role, sophisticated and long-endurance drones'.[58] The government

---

49. Pradip R Sagar, 'Indo-US Arms Embrace', *India Today*, 21 March 2023, <https://www.indiatoday.in/magazine/defence/story/20230327-indo-us-arms-embrace-2347499-2023-03-17>, accessed 1 April 2023.
50. Aritra Banerjee, 'US, Russia and France Vying for Indian Arms Market as India Moves Towards Strategic Self-Reliance', *Indian Aerospace and Defence Bulletin*, 13 March 2023, <https://www.iadb.in/2023/03/13/us-russia-france-vying-for-indian-arms-market-as-india-moves-towards-strategic-self-reliance/>, accessed 1 April 2023.
51. *Diplomacy and Beyond*, 'At Aero India 2023, India and Israel to Boost their Defence Ties on Aerial Frontiers', 10 February 2023, <https://diplomacybeyond.com/at-aero-india-2023-india-and-israel-to-boost-their-defence-ties-on-aerial-frontiers/>, accessed 1 April 2023.
52. Colonel Balwan Singh Nagial, 'Atmanirbhar Bharat and Self-Reliance in Defence', *Times of India*, 2 May 2022, <https://timesofindia.indiatimes.com/blogs/col-nagial/atmanirbhar-bharat-and-self-reliance-in-defence/>, accessed 25 October 2022.
53. *Economic Times*, 'Defence Ministry Nod for Purchase of Rs 76,000 Crore India-made Equipment', 6 June 2022, <https://economictimes.indiatimes.com/news/defence/defence-ministry-nod-for-purchase-of-rs-76000-crore-india-made-equipment/articleshow/92045285.cms>, accessed 18 July 2022.
54. Dalip Singh, 'Defence Ministry to Unveil Atmanirbhar Bharat-II for Indigenous Production of Core Technologies', *Hindu Buisnessline*, 2 August 2022, <https://www.thehindubusinessline.com/news/national/defence-ministry-to-unveil-atmanirbhar-bharat-ii-for-indigenous-production-of-core-technologies/article65716952.ece>, accessed 25 October 2022.
55. Huma Siddiqui, 'PM Modi's Boost for Atmanirbhar Bharat in Defence Sector; Seven New Companies Dedicated to the Nation', *Financial Express*, 15 October 2021, <https://www.financialexpress.com/defence/pm-modis-boost-for-atmanirbhar-bharat-in-defence-sector-seven-new-companies-dedicated-to-the-nation/2350490/>, accessed 25 October 2022.
56. *Hindustan Times*, 'Indian Army Eyes Major Firepower Upgrade to Counter China', 27 September 2022, <https://www.hindustantimes.com/india-news/indian-army-eyes-major-firepower-upgrade-to-counter-china-101664280649581.html>, accessed 25 October 2022.
57. Pradip R Sagar, 'Lessons for India from Russia-Ukraine conflict', *The Week*, 3 June 2022, <https://www.theweek.in/news/india/2022/06/03/lessons-for-india-from-russia-ukraine-conflict.html>, accessed 25 October 2022.
58. *Mint*, 'For Vigil over LAC, India Develops AI-Driven Drone. Read Here', 7 August 2022, <https://www.livemint.com/news/india/for-vigil-over-lac-india-develops-ai-driven-drone-read-here-11659869620462.html>, accessed 25 October 2022.

has roped in the private sector too; the DRDO in partnership with the Tata and the Kalyani Group is developing the 155 mm, 52 calibre Advanced Towed Artillery Gun System (ATAGS).[59] Since the acquisition of defence equipment is a drawn out process, the Indian army has sought to 'fast track' the procedure for procurement of Logistic Drones.[60] Effectively, the Modi regime has pushed the mantra of being 'atmanirbhar'. However, the performance of PSUs in India remains a question mark, and their ability to deliver 'quality' goods continues to be a matter of concern.[61]

Russia–China Relations

However, the key long-term concern for New Delhi that arises from the war in Ukraine is the growing camaraderie between Moscow and Beijing. While Beijing may have 'questions' about the war in Ukraine, the two countries are bound together with a common goal, that is, to establish a new world order.[62] According to Shullman and Taylor, the growing coordination between the two countries on security matters and efforts to shape the global order complicates the strategic challenges for the US and its allies.[63] The 'no limits' relationship is bound to create ripples across the Western world and have major implications for India.[64] Bilateral trade between Russia and China is expected to touch a new high of $170 billion.[65] New Delhi is worried that as the war drags on, Russia will eventually become China's 'junior partner'.[66] India's National Security Advisor, Ajit Doval, reportedly informed his Russian counterpart that New Delhi has never been committed to a single camp and has always prioritised its own self-interest, while also being worried about Russia's drift toward China.[67] From New Delhi's perspective, in the long term even if Russia is weak, it would still be expected to have enough diplomatic prowess to pressure governments to preserve peace along the borders and stability in South Asia.

After over 12 months of conflict, it is evident that Western sanctions have affected the Russian military industrial complex.[68] Given the challenges for Moscow, it seems likely that Russia will outsource more of its hardware production to China. As a consequence, the procurement of weapons and their related spare parts from Russia will be a major problem for New Delhi in the coming years. Although the Modi regime has strengthened its fences, geostrategic challenges along the LAC and Line of Control (LoC) continue to test the military capabilities

59. Ajai Shukla, Devangshu Datta and Bhaswar Kumar, 'How Atmanirbhar is India When it Comes to Defence?', *Business Standard*, 21 October 2022, <https://www.business-standard.com/podcast/current-affairs/how-atmanirbhar-is-india-when-it-comes-to-defence-122102100234_1.html>, accessed 25 October 2022.
60. Mayank Singh, 'Indian Army to Buy 363 High and Medium Altitude Drones', *New Indian Express*, 18 October 2022, <https://www.newindianexpress.com/nation/2022/oct/18/indian-army-to-buy-363-high--medium-altitude-drones-2509296.html>, accessed 25 October 2022.
61. SN Misra, 'The Myth of Atmanirbhar Bharat in Defence Manufacturing', *The Wire*, 11 October 2021, <https://thewire.in/political-economy/the-myth-of-atmanirbhar-bharat-in-defence-manufacturing>, accessed 25 October 2022.
62. Nectar Gan, 'Xi and Putin Want to Create a New World Order. Russia's Setback in Ukraine could Spoil their Plans', *CNN*, 15 September 2022.
63. David O Shullman and Andrea Kendall-Taylor, 'Best and Bosom Friends: Why China-Russia Ties Will Deepen after Russia's War on Ukraine', *Marshall Papers*, CSIS Briefs, <https://csis-website-prod.s3.amazonaws.com/s3fs-public/publication/220622_Shullman_BestBosomFriends_ChinaRussia.pdf?CqUu5rbqXbj2p5YT2EXBeY9E1jYJak3C>, accessed 25 October 2022.
64. Elizabeth Wishnick, 'The China–Russia 'No Limits' Partnership is still Going Strong, with Regime Security as Top Priority', *South China Morning Post*, 29 September 2022, <https://www.scmp.com/comment/opinion/article/3193703/china-russia-no-limits-partnership-still-going-strong-regime>, accessed 25 October 2022.
65. Cheng Li, 'Evolving China-Russia Relations: A Major Challenge for Xi's Third Term', *The Reshuffling Report*, 3 October 2022, <https://www.chinausfocus.com/2022-CPC-congress/evolving-china-russia-relations-a-major-challenge-for-xis-third-term>, accessed 25 October 2022.
66. *Mint*, 'SCO Summit: Putin Meets Xi, Praises China's "Balanced" Approach', 16 September 2022, <https://www.livemint.com/news/world/sco-summit-putin-meets-xi-praises-china-s-balanced-approach-11663311094340.html>, accessed 25 October 2022.
67. Shishir Gupta, 'India Exercises Strategic Autonomy, Worried at Russia's "No Limit" China Tilt', *Hindustan Times*, 19 August 2022, <https://www.hindustantimes.com/india-news/india-exercises-strategic-autonomy-worried-at-russia-s-china-tilt-101660874108079.html>, accessed 25 October 2022.
68. US Department of State, 'The Impact of Sanctions and Export Controls on the Russian Federation', 20 October 2022, <https://www.state.gov/the-impact-of-sanctions-and-export-controls-on-the-russian-federation/>, accessed 25 October 2022.

of India from time to time. The Modi government, which has started a loud campaign against Pakistan and China, cannot afford to lower its guard along India's borders as long as the situation remains unstable. For the Modi regime, Chinese belligerence along the LAC and its 'ironclad friendship'[69] with Pakistan is a matter of concern. Equally worrying is Moscow's growing warmth towards the OIC[70] where statements sponsored by Pakistan on Kashmir are frequently passed.[71] Recently, Moscow and Beijing have increased their economic engagement with the Taliban in Afghanistan, which has left New Delhi in a challenging position.[72]

Saturated Ties with the West?

India's stance on the Ukraine conflict will undoubtedly have a long-term impact on its relationship with the US and its key allies. For the West, a democratic India is seen as a natural partner. However, New Delhi's 'shaky' stand has left the West perplexed.[73] Despite numerous European foreign ministers visiting India in the wake of Russia's invasion of Ukraine, External Affairs Minister Jaishankar was quick to counsel the West that India was not sitting on the fence and was allowed to have its own viewpoint.[74] Again, at a forum in Slovakia, he also said, 'Europe has to grow out of the mindset that Europe's problems are the world's problems but the world's problems are not Europe's problems'.[75] A deeper analysis will reveal that India's approach to the war has less to do with its historical and defence connections with Russia and more with the saturation of ties with the West. New Delhi clearly expects more from the West, unconditionally. While cooperation with the West in several key sectors has moved upwards, a 'rising India'[76] is no longer satisfied with the current state of relations. The surge in trade relations, collaboration in science and technology, advancement of capitalism and consumer industries, and partnership space exploration have ensured that this minimum threshold of cooperation has been realised. Furthermore, presence of a 'democratic culture' and large Indian diaspora across the West has all added strength to this relationship. After achieving this threshold level, India's relations with the West have plateaued. For both parties, there is a growing realisation that mutual relationship is unlikely to fall below this threshold level and the chances are that it can grow rather positively.

For the US and its allies in the Indo-Pacific region, China has emerged as the biggest long-term threat; New Delhi too is worried about China's lurking presence in South Asia and its neighbourhood. From Washington's perspective, China is the only country that has the economic, political, military and technical might to pose a long-term threat to an open and stable international order.[77] Alignment of interests is clearly visible for India and the US; for New Delhi, not Pakistan but China has been identified as the key adversary[78]

69. Nong Rong, 'China and Pakistan Iron-clad Friendship is Rock-solid, *Daily Times*, 21 May 2022, <https://dailytimes.com.pk/938378/china-and-pakistan-iron-clad-friendship-is-rock-solid/>, accessed 25 October 2022.
70. *TASS*, 'Lavrov to Hold Talks with OIC Head in Moscow Next Week – Russian Foreign Ministry', 21 October 2022, <https://tass.com/politics/1525955>, accessed 25 October 2022.
71. Rezaul H Laskar, 'India Rejects OIC Statement on Jammu and Kashmir', *Hindustan Times*, 6 August 2022, <https://www.hindustantimes.com/india-news/india-rejects-oic-statement-on-jammu-and-kashmir-101659724460364.html>, accessed 25 October 2022.
72. Michael Schollon, 'Taliban-Russia Deal a Drop in the Bucket that Could Fuel Future Trade', *Radio Free Europe/Radio Liberty*, 5 October 2022, <https://www.rferl.org/a/afghanistan-russia-taliban-fuel-deal/32066483.html>, accessed 25 October 2022.
73. Prashant Jha and Rezaul H Laskar, 'India "Shaky" on Ukraine War: Joe Biden', *Hindustan Times*, 23 March 2022, <https://www.hindustantimes.com/india-news/india-shaky-on-ukraine-war-biden-101647973402819.html>, accessed 16 July 2022.
74. *Hindustan Times*, '"No, India not Sitting on Fence": Jaishankar Says Europe has to Change Mindset", 3 June 2022, <https://www.hindustantimes.com/india-news/no-india-not-sitting-on-fence-jaishankar-says-europe-has-to-change-mindset-101654245499431.html>, accessed 25 October 2022.
75. Sourav Roy Barman, 'Europe has to Grow out of Mindset that its Problems are World's Problems: Jaishankar', *Indian Express*, 4 June 2022, <https://indianexpress.com/article/india/europe-has-to-grow-out-of-mindset-that-its-problems-are-worlds-problems-jaishankar-7951895/>, accessed 14 July 2022.
76. Rajesh Basrur and Kate Sullivan de Estrada, *Rising India: Status & Power* (London: Routledge, 2017).
77. The White House, 'Interim National Security Strategic Guidance', March 2021, <https://www.whitehouse.gov/wp-content/uploads/2021/03/NSC-1v2.pdf>, accessed 18 July 2022.
78. Olav Albuquerque, 'China was Always India's Enemy No.1', *The Bridge Chronicle*, 19 June 2020, <https://www.thebridgechronicle.com/opinion/china-was-always-india%E2%80%99s-enemy-no1-51998>, accessed 17 July 2022.

and as such would 'never accept a Sino-centric Asia'.[79] To guarantee stability in the Indo-Pacific region and to counter China's looming threats, the Quad will need to become more 'muscular'. However, contradictions between India and other members of the Quad are quite apparent; for India, challenges in the Indo-Pacific region are more economically driven than security-oriented. Essentially, the 'robustness' of the Quad has been weakened by New Delhi's ambivalent approach towards the Indo-Pacific region. India has sent a very clear message to the West that its engagement with multilateral institutions will be driven by national interest. Furthermore, India's participation in the Shanghai Cooperation Organisation (SCO), an institution which has transformed from being 'non-West' to 'anti-West', has not gone down too well in Washington.[80]

When compared with other Asian economies, India is doing exceptionally well, with projected economic growth of 7.3% for the current fiscal year.[81] New Delhi recognises that as the world's fifth biggest economy, the West can no longer overlook India's presence.[82] As seen by the exemption of India from Countering America's Adversaries through Sanctions Act (CAATSA), Washington wants India to remain outside of the Russia–China ambit.[83] Unilateral sanctions will not limit but rather strengthen New Delhi's behaviour. For the Modi government, everything 'foreign' needs to be questioned, and this narrative is gaining traction in India. As politicians mostly talk about nationalism and patriotism, there is added pressure on the Modi regime to show the people that India is an equal partner of the West and not one that is subservient to it.[84] New Delhi's balancing act has impeded, but not derailed, its relations with the West.

Limits of the Balancing Act

Modi's administration has stressed that 'today's era is not an era of war'.[85] At a time when most Western countries have imposed economic sanctions on Russia, India has kept its window open for trade with Moscow. India's balancing act will continue to prevail until it reaches its 'tipping point', importantly in favour of the West as relations between the parties have crossed the minimum threshold of cooperation. Despite complementary and at times contradictory interests, the multifaceted relationship between Western liberal democracies and India is too deep to be easily uprooted. Undoubtedly, there are numerous variables that may move India away from Russia in the long term, most of them are connected to its national security, territorial integrity and developments in South Asia. If Russia begins to revisit India's 'core' national interests, which include questioning India's territorial integrity, particularly the locus standi of Jammu and Kashmir, endorsing China's position on Arunachal Pradesh, which Beijing refers to as 'South Tibet',[86] ignoring the activities of anti-India terror groups in Afghanistan and Pakistan, questioning the state of governance in the country, interrogating controversial acts such as the Citizenship Amendment Act (CAA) and the abrogation of Article 370,[87] as well as reevaluating India's claim for a permanent seat in the UN Security

79. C Raja Mohan, 'India: Between "Strategic Autonomy" and "Geopolitical Opportunity"', *Asia Policy* (No. 15, January 2013), p. 24.
80. PS Raghavan, 'Does India Belong in the SCO', *New Indian Express*, 14 September 2022, <https://www.newindianexpress.com/opinions/2022/sep/14/does-india-belong-in-the-sco-2497905.html>, accessed 25 October 2022.
81. *Business Today*, 'S&P Global Projects India's GDP Growth at 7.3% in 2022-23, 6.5% for Next Fiscal', 26 September 2022, <https://www.businesstoday.in/latest/economy/story/sp-global-projects-indias-gdp-growth-at-73-in-2022-23-65-for-next-fiscal-348167-2022-09-26>, accessed 25 October 2022.
82. *The Hindu*, 'India Overtakes UK to Become Fifth Largest Economy in the World', 3 September 2022, <https://www.thehindu.com/news/national/india-overtakes-uk-to-become-fifth-largest-economy-in-the-world/article65844906.ece>, accessed 25 October 2022.
83. Rishika Singh, 'Explained: US Exempts India from CAATSA, What is it?', *Indian Express*, 15 July 2022, <https://indianexpress.com/article/explained/us-caatsa-india-russia-s400-missile-weapons-system-8016536/>, accessed 25 October 2022.
84. Richard N Haass, 'Economic Sanctions: Too Much of a Bad Thing', *Brookings*, 1 June 1998, <https://www.brookings.edu/research/economic-sanctions-too-much-of-a-bad-thing/>, accessed 25 October 2022.
85. Shubhajit Roy, 'Not Era of War, PM tells Putin Who says Will Try to End Ukraine Conflict Soonest', *Indian Express*, 17 September 2022, <https://indianexpress.com/article/world/indian-pm-modi-tells-russias-putin-now-is-not-an-era-war-8155737/>, accessed 25 October 2022.
86. K J M Varma, 'China Says Arunachal Pradesh Part of It "Since Ancient Times"', *The Print*, 31 December 2021, <https://theprint.in/diplomacy/china-says-arunachal-pradesh-part-of-it-since-ancient-times/792565/>, accessed 1 April 2023.
87. Article 370 of the Constitution of India provided for 'temporary, transitional and special provisions' for the state of Jammu and Kashmir. It was abrogated in August 2019.

Council (UNSC), then New Delhi may very well move out of Moscow's ambit.

While long-term factors may impact Russia–India ties, given the circumstances, Moscow would be foolish to revisit such issues in the near future. Unlike the West, Moscow has seldom questioned India's domestic policies. India has sought to strengthen relations with Moscow knowing that it will make the West squirm a little. For its part, the West is gradually tightening the screws on New Delhi. In September 2022, India lashed out at the Biden administration for approving the $450 million F-16 fighter jet fleet sustainment programme to Pakistan.[88] Despite being the 'epicentre of global terrorism',[89] Pakistan has also been removed from the FATF grey list.[90] Both these issues show that New Delhi and Washington are not on the same page. Consequently, in the future, Washington may continue to be ambivalent about India's bid for a permanent seat on the UNSC in light of India's stance on a number of critical issues.[91]

In spite of being 'strategic partners', the India–US defence cooperation continues to be rather muted. Bishoyi argues that the future of the India–US strategic partnership will, to a large extent, depend on 'technology transfer and co-production of high techs in defence and strategic sectors'.[92] While the Biden administration is preparing to provide India $500 million in military aid to lessen New Delhi's reliance on Moscow, it may not be enough. India is seeking further investment from the US and the EU to reach a $5 trillion GDP by 2024–25.[93] However, what New Delhi really wants is for the West to stay out of India's domestic issues and not comment on sensitive topics such as rising Hindu nationalism and the rights of minorities. According to the Modi government, international rankings on issues like hunger, human rights and press freedom that are compiled by so-called 'Western' organisations, are meant to 'sully' India's reputation.[94] Washington – and the Democrats in particular[95] – is very critical of the Modi regime and questions India's domestic policies, in contrast to Moscow, which has never expressed interest in India's internal affairs. The West realises that such questions may make the Modi government uncomfortable and slow down the pace of cooperation, but it cannot change the course of relations between the two countries. Because of India's volatile neighbourhood and the perpetual election environment, the West also understands that the Modi administration may take a stance which challenges its position. However, given the strong anti-Pakistan and anti-China sentiments prevailing in the country, the Modi regime can ill afford to publicly support any initiative spearheaded by Beijing and Islamabad. For the Modi government, the last thing it wants is to be seen as 'weak' by India's electorate.

88. *The Hindu*, 'Biden Administration Approves $450 million F-16 Fleet Sustainment Programme to Pakistan', 8 September 2022, <https://www.thehindu.com/news/international/biden-administration-approves-450-million-f-16-fleet-sustainment-programme-to-pakistan/article65864895.ece>, accessed 25 October 2022.
89. Suhasini Haidar, 'At Kazakhstan Meeting, India Terms Pakistan Epicentre of Terrorism', *The Hindu*, 13 October 2022, <https://www.thehindu.com/news/national/india-desires-normal-relations-with-all-its-neighbours-including-pakistan-mos-lekhi/article66005482.ece>, accessed 25 October 2022.
90. *Times of India*, 'Pakistan Removed from FATF Grey List on Terror Financing', 22 October 2022, <https://timesofindia.indiatimes.com/world/pakistan/pakistan-removed-from-fatf-grey-list-on-terror-financing/articleshow/95021064.cms>, accessed 25 October 2022.
91. Sriram Lakshman, 'Biden Administration Non-committal on Support for Permanent UNSC Seat for India', *The Hindu*, 6 August 2021, <https://www.thehindu.com/news/international/biden-administration-non-committal-on-support-for-permanent-unsc-seat-for-india/article35757993.ece>, accessed 25 October 2022.
92. Saroj Bishoyi, 'India-US Forging Tech Alliance since Long. Now Use 2+2 Dialogue to Push it Further', *The Print*, 11 April 2022, <https://theprint.in/opinion/india-us-forging-tech-alliance-since-long-now-use-22-dialogue-to-push-it-further/910983/>, accessed 18 July 2022.
93. *Economic Times*, 'India Would Become $5-trillion Economy by 2026-27: CEA V Anantha Nageswaran', 14 June 2022, <https://economictimes.indiatimes.com/news/economy/indicators/india-would-become-5-trillion-economy-by-2026-27-cea-v-anantha-nageswaran/articleshow/92205688.cms>, accessed 17 July 2022.
94. Jagriti Chandra, 'Global Hunger Index Attempt to Tarnish India's Image: Centre', *The Hindu*, 15 October 2022, <https://www.thehindu.com/news/national/global-hunger-index-attempt-to-tarnish-indias-image-centre/article66015191.ece>, accessed 25 October 2022.
95. Chidanand Rajghatta, 'Rift between Progressive Democrats in US and Modi Government Out in the Open', *Times of India*, 20 December 2019, <https://timesofindia.indiatimes.com/world/us/rift-between-progressive-democrats-in-us-and-modi-government-out-in-open/articleshow/72897482.cms>, accessed 1 April 2023.

Conclusion

India's stand on the war in Ukraine has renewed the debate on 'neutrality' and 'hedging' in a fluid world order. As the global economic and food crises loom large, several countries in the Middle East, Africa and Asia too have acted cautiously; rather, they have been reluctant to condemn Russia and follow the diktats of the US. For many such developing countries, the lure of cheaper oil at 'discounted rates' from Russia is simply too good a proposition to be ignored. Not only has the war in Ukraine exposed the gap between the Global North and the Global South,[96] contrary to expectations of the West, more countries of the developing world are gravitating towards Russia.[97] For many of the developing countries, NATO is to be blamed for the war in Ukraine.[98] However, India's pro-Russian stance runs much deeper than defence ties and economic reasons alone. If the past is anything to go by, despite regional and strategic challenges, the camaraderie between Moscow and New Delhi is firmly established. When the West refused or was reluctant to help, the Soviet Union stepped in; according to Jaishankar, such strong defence relations with Moscow arose as a result of the West failing to provide India with meaningful defence equipment.[99] Russia has used its veto in the UN to bail out India on several occasions.[100] Furthermore, Russia remains a 'crucial partner' of India that can help it reach its nuclear energy potential.[101] Thus, political leaders and the Indian public hold Russia in high esteem for its support of India's cause. Domestic and electoral compulsions also influence India's pro-Russia position. Voting behaviour in India is seldom influenced by foreign policy, with the exception of matters relating to terrorism, Pakistan and China.[102] The Rashtriya Swayamsevak Sangh (RSS), which has an 'organic link' with the Bharatiya Janata Party (BJP),[103] has spread its Hindutva-nationalist agenda among India's sizeable middle class, which is also sensitive to the West's 'hypocrisy' on issues of oil purchases from Russia,[104] 'war' and 'territorial integrity'. Additionally, External Affairs Minister Jaishankar has pointed out that the West has adopted a soft approach towards Pakistan, which he calls the 'epicentre of terrorism'.[105] For the vast majority of the population, the ability of the Modi regime to question the actions of the West rather than Moscow represents a symbolic victory, for it signals India's 'muscular'[106] approach to world politics and its ability

96. Leela Jacinto, 'Ukraine War Exposes Splits between Global North and South', *France 24*, 17 February 2023, <https://www.france24.com/en/europe/20230217-ukraine-war-exposes-splits-between-global-north-and-south>, accessed 1 April 2023.
97. Elliot Smith, '"It's Not a Pretty Picture": Russia's Support is Growing in the Developing World', *CNBC*, 30 March 2023, <https://www.cnbc.com/2023/03/30/ukraine-war-how-russias-support-is-growing-in-the-developing-world.html>, accessed 1 April 2023.
98. Liz Sly, 'A Global Divide on the Ukraine War is Deepening', *Washington Post*, 23 February 2023.
99. *Indian Express*, 'Dependence on Russian Defence Equipment not Lack of Trying on India's Part: Jaishankar', 26 September 2022, <https://indianexpress.com/article/india/dependence-russian-defence-equipment-lack-trying-indias-part-jaishankar-8173144/>, accessed 25 October 2022.
100. In the past, on several occasions, Russia has used its veto in the UNSC to prevent discussion of the 'India-Pakistan question'. For details, see Christopher Snedden, 'India-Russia: A Friend in Need', *The Interpreter*, 22 April 2022, <https://www.lowyinstitute.org/the-interpreter/india-russia-friend-need>, accessed 1 April 2023.
101. Shailendra Deolankar, 'Nuclear Energy: A Critical Pillar Enriching India–Russia Relationship', *Businessworld*, 9 April 2021, <https://www.businessworld.in/article/Nuclear-Energy-A-Critical-Pillar-Enriching-India-Russia-Relationship/09-04-2021-386157/>, accessed 13 July 2022.
102. Prashant Kumar Choudhary, Reetika Syal and Tarun Arora, 'Do Issues Matter in Indian Elections?', *Indian Politics & Policy* (Vol. 3, No. 1, 2020), pp. 31–48.
103. Arun Anand, 'How and Why the Relationship Between RSS and BJP has Worked so Well', *Firstpost*, 28 May 2022, <https://www.firstpost.com/opinion/right-word-how-and-why-the-relationship-between-rss-and-bjp-has-worked-so-well-10729191.html>, accessed 1 April 2023.
104. Shi Lancha and Chen Anlan, 'Why Did Jaishankar's Speech Suddenly Become Popular in China?', *Global Times*, 9 June 2022, <https://www.globaltimes.cn/page/202206/1267699.shtml>, accessed 1 April 2023.
105. *Indian Express*, '"Could Use Harsher Words...": Jaishankar on Use of Phrase "Epicentre of Terrorism" for Pakistan', 3 January 2023, <https://indianexpress.com/article/india/could-use-harsher-words-jaishankar-use-phrase-epicentre-terrorism-for-pakistan-8358436/>, accessed 1 April 2023.
106. Jyoti Malhotra, 'In Naya MEA, why Jaishankar's Cool Quotient and India's Muscular Foreign Policy are Similar', *The Print*, 22 February 2022, <https://theprint.in/opinion/global-print/in-naya-mea-why-jaishankars-cool-quotient-and-indias-muscular-foreign-policy-are-similar/841358/>, accessed 25 October 2022.

to shackle off the chains of colonialism. As a result, the Russia–India connection will endure regardless of the outcome of the Ukrainian conflict or the health of the defence partnership.

Notwithstanding their positions on hard security issues, India and the West will have to live together despite a growing discomfort. Due to their extensive economic ties and mutual respect for one another's soft power, relations between India and the West cannot fall below a certain degree of partnership. The course of India–Russia relations is dependent on a number of factors; the ball is squarely in Moscow's court. Since the border confrontations with China in the Galwan Valley, the Indian government has 'mirror' deployed its military personnel to guarantee that future hostilities stay limited to the high Himalayas. In the past two years, India's military and border infrastructure has been substantially upgraded.[107] Thus, India has emerged as a contrarian power with ample strength to withstand global pressure and decide its own course of action.

In recent years, there has been a dramatic shift in India's perspective on great power competition and world security. India's foreign policy is now marked by 'strategic hedging'. It exemplifies a period in which New Delhi will steadfastly defend its national interests in different multilateral forums and frameworks. If history is any guide, it can be expected that India will strive to protect its national interest and will not engage in anyone else's war until its own borders and sovereignty are endangered. As things are, expecting New Delhi to participate in any military burden-sharing advocated by the West is pointless. For the time being, Russia and India have opted not to upset the status quo of their longstanding ties. ■

Shubhrajeet Konwer is an Associate Professor at Gauhati University's Department of Political Science. He received his Masters and MPhil degrees from the School of International Studies at Jawaharlal Nehru University in New Delhi, as well as his PhD from Gauhati University. His articles on India's foreign policy have been published in *Strategic Analysis* and the *International Journal of China Studies*.

107. Bharti Jain, 'Major Upgrade for India Infrastructure Along LAC: Parliamentary Panel Report', *Times of India*, 15 March 2022, <https://timesofindia.indiatimes.com/india/47-new-itbp-border-outposts-being-created-along-china-border/articleshow/90211881.cms>, accessed 25 October 2022.

Research Article
RUSI Journal

Studying Moscow's Coercive Campaign Against Norway

The Bear is Awake

Runar Spansvoll

Norway's geopolitical position as both a neighbour of Russia and a member of NATO places it at the forefront of Moscow's self-assertive and aggressive foreign and security policy. However, Norway's NATO membership reduces Russia's room for manoeuvre to actions below the threshold of armed conflict. In this article, Runar Spansvoll examines how Russia has made use of such aggressive and coercive sub-threshold activities in the political, information and military domains between 2014–23 in a campaign to compel Oslo to comply with its foreign and security policy objectives.

Russia's increasingly self-assertive and revisionist foreign and security policy may not have received sufficient attention in the West until the sudden and illegal annexation of Crimea in 2014. Although the seizure sent geopolitical shockwaves into capitals around the world, the subsequent political response did not deter President Vladimir Putin from attempting to subjugate the whole of Ukraine in 2022. These two watershed events – the latter of which is still unfolding – have led to an almost complete collapse in relations with the West, including Norway, one of Russia's immediate neighbours.

From Norway's perspective, the deterioration in bilateral relations since 2014 has been visible through the degradation of political dialogue, cases of espionage, cyber attacks and a substantial increase in coercive military activity, as described in the following sections. From the Russian perspective, its security concerns related to Norway seem primarily linked to Norway's administration and use of Svalbard, the presence of NATO forces in Norway and in its adjoining seas, and the Norwegian sanctions policy. Historically, these matters have been insufficient cause for escalation as Russia has had an enduring interest in 'preserving the Arctic as a territory of peace', isolated from conflicts elsewhere.[1] Nevertheless, Russia's renewed invasion of Ukraine makes it evident that its risk perception and acceptance exceeds traditional parameters, making its foreign policy conduct and role as an actor in the international system unpredictable.

This article explores Moscow's campaign to influence and coerce Oslo into complying with its foreign and security policy objectives in the timeframe between 2014 and early 2023. These efforts can be grouped into the political, information and military domains where activities have remained under the threshold for armed conflict. Although the primary focus of this article is on Norway, it is important to recognise that Russia's actions are not isolated incidents. Indeed, several of the actions taken by Russia against Norway are reflective of its broader patterns of behaviour towards other

1. President of the Russian Federation, 'Ukaz Prezidenta Rossijskoj Federacii ot 26.10.2020 # 645 "O Strategii razvitija Arkticheskoj zony Rossijskoj Federacii i obespechenija nacional'noj bezopasnosti na period do 2035 goda"' ['On the Strategy for the Development of the Arctic Zone of the Russian Federation and Ensuring National Security for the Period up to 2035'], 26 October 2020, <http://actual.pravo.gov.ru/text.html#pnum=0001202010260033>, accessed 27 April 2023, p. 16.

 © The Author, Vol. 168, No. 3, 2023 pp. 74 85

A Norwegian F-35 A on NATO Quick Reaction Alert intercepting a Russian TU-95MS 'BEAR-H' near Norwegian airspace. *Courtesy of Forsvaret / Norwegian Armed Forces*

NATO partners. Therefore, this article should be considered a case study in Russian coercive actions to influence political decision-making, highlighting the comprehensive nature of Moscow's disruptive actions and contributing to increased awareness of the wider phenomenon.

Diplomacy: Norway is a Member of NATO; NATO is not a Friend of Russia

Russia's illegal annexation of Crimea in 2014 is considered a turning point in Russo-Norwegian relations. Shortly after the annexation, Norway implemented sanctions in line with those of the EU. In turn, Russia is believed to have orchestrated the subsequent refugee crisis at the Russo-Norwegian border crossing station in Storskog in the last quarter of 2015. According to former prime minister Erna Solberg, Russia did this by assisting or allowing more than 5,000 refugees from various conflict zones to seek asylum at the border.[2] This represented a significant increase compared with the first half of 2015, when only 40 people applied for asylum at the border.[3] The situation bears similarities to the 2021 migration crisis on the border between the EU and Belarus, where Alexander Lukashenko's regime used illegal immigration as a political weapon in response to Western and EU sanctions.[4]

In another instance of political manoeuvring, Russia's Foreign Minister Sergey Lavrov used the 2020 centenary of the Svalbard Treaty to formally protest violations of the treaty on the grounds of discrimination against Russian economic activity in the archipelago, demanding bilateral negotiations. However, Oslo dismissed the demand on the

2. *Nettavisen*, 'Solberg: Russland lot migranter strømme på for å teste Norges respons' ['Solberg: Russia Allowed Migrants to Pour in to Test Norway's Response'], 23 September 2021, <https://www.nettavisen.no/nyheter/solberg-russland-lot-migranter-stromme-pa-for-a-teste-norges-respons/s/12-95-3424182766>, accessed 27 April 2023.
3. Norwegian Directorate of Immigration, 'Tall og fakta 2015' ['Numbers and Facts 2015'], 25 February 2016, pp. 12–13, <https://www.udi.no/en/statistics-and-analysis/facts-and-figures/tall-og-fakta-2015>, accessed 27 April 2023.
4. Brian Whitmore, 'Belarus Dictator Weaponizes Illegal Migrants Against EU', Atlantic Council, 30 June 2021, <https://www.atlanticcouncil.org/blogs/belarusalert/belarus-dictator-weaponizes-illegal-migrants-against-eu/>, accessed 20 September 2022.

DOI: 10.1080/03071847.2023.2220756

grounds that 'Norway does not negotiate with anyone over what is Norwegian', causing outrage in the Russian media.[5] Although the protest was based on allegations of economic discrimination against Russia's symbolic Arktikugol coal mining company in Barentsburg, the underlying concern was likely related to the geostrategic location of Svalbard in relation to Russia's strategic nuclear forces on the Kola Peninsula. That is also why the Svalbard satellite station (SvalSat) has been criticised by Russian officials who claim that the facility serves dual-use purposes.[6] SvalSat is operated by the part government-owned Kongsberg Satellite Services (KSAT) and the Norwegian Space Agency and is vital in communicating with satellites in low polar orbit.

In May 2021, the Russian Embassy in Oslo openly criticised Norway for alleged violations of its self-imposed 1949 basing policy, which includes restrictions on foreign military presence in Norway.[7] Specifically, the Embassy stated that Norway had allowed US nuclear attack submarines and strategic bombers to use Norwegian ports and airports, which it argued violated the 1949 policy.[8] The Embassy also criticised the 2021 US-Norwegian Supplementary Defense Cooperation Agreement (SDCA), which grants the US increased jurisdiction over its military personnel and infrastructure within defined areas in Norway, enables joint training and exercises, sharing of military infrastructure and technology, and cooperation on security challenges.[9]

Relations deteriorated further on 25 October 2021, when Lavrov met with his newly appointed Norwegian counterpart, Anniken Huitfeldt. In the subsequent statement to the press, he announced that 'Norway is a member of NATO, and NATO is not a friend of Russia'.[10] Lavrov's statement represented continuity in de facto relations since 2014, however, his directness in challenging the cornerstone of Norwegian security policy signalled change.

Following Russia's attempted full-scale invasion of Ukraine in 2022, Norway implemented sanctions mirroring those of the EU, and continues to supply Ukraine with military hardware and funds. This resulted in Moscow listing Norway as a 'nation unfriendly to Russia'.[11] In addition, in July 2022 Russian politicians suggested invalidating the much-celebrated 2010 Russo-Norwegian maritime delimitation treaty – the result of four decades of negotiations – as an indirect, punitive response to Norwegian sanctions. The reaction from the Norwegian Ministry of Foreign Affairs has so far been that the treaty does not have a clause on termination.[12]

Despite the entrenched political positions, the Norwegian Intelligence Service (NIS) assesses that Moscow considers its diplomatic means the most

5. Atle Staalesen, 'Norway's Celebration of the Svalbard Treaty was Followed by an Ardent and Coordinated Response from Moscow Media', *Barents Observer*, 2 July 2020, <https://thebarentsobserver.com/en/2020/07/norways-celebration-svalbard-treaty-was-followed-ardent-and-coordinated-response-moscow>, accessed 29 April 2023; Russia's Ministry of Foreign Affairs, 'On Russian Reservations Towards the Svalbard Treaty', 4 February 2020, <https://archive.mid.ru/web/guest/maps/no/-/asset_publisher/f4MKo6byouc4/content/id/4019093>, accessed 29 April 2023.
6. Mathieu Boulègue, *Russia's Military Posture in the Arctic – Managing Hard Power in a "Low Tension" Environment* (Lodon: Royal Institute of International Affairs, 2019), p. 27; see also Thomas Nilsen, 'Russia Complains of Norwegian Navy's Visit to Svalbard', *Arctic Today*, 15 November 2021, <https://www.arctictoday.com/russia-complains-of-norwegian-navys-visit-to-svalbard/>, accessed 4 March 2022.
7. Olav Riste, 'Isolasjonisme og stormaktsgarantier' ['Isolationism and Great Power Guarantees'], 1991, pp. 23–30, <https://fhs.brage.unit.no/fhs-xmlui/handle/11250/99455>, accessed 29 April 2023.
8. The Russian Embassy in Oslo, 'Om anløp av amerikanske atomubåter til Tønsneshavn ved Tromsø' ['On American Nuclear Submarines to Tønsneshavn near Tromsø'], 18 May 2021, <https://norway.mid.ru/no/embassy/press-centre/news/?PAGEN_1=3&>, accessed 29 April 2023.
9. Nilsen, 'Russia Complains of Norwegian Navy's Visit to Svalbard'; The Norwegian Government, 'Norway Signs Supplementary Defense Cooperation Agreement with the United States', 16 April 2021, <https://www.regjeringen.no/en/aktuelt/undertegner-tilleggsavtale-om-forsvarssamarbeid-med-usa/id2844970/>, accessed 29 April 2023.
10. Hilde-Gunn Bye, 'Lavrov: We Do Not have Relations with NATO, but We have with Norway', *High North News*, 26 October 2021, <https://www.highnorthnews.com/en/lavrov-we-do-not-have-relations-nato-we-have-norway>, accessed 8 February 2022.
11. *Tass*, 'Kabmin utverdil perechen' nedruzhestvennyh Rossii stran i territorij' ['The Cabinet of Ministers Approved the List of Countries and Territories Unfriendly to Russia'], 7 March 2022.
12. NRK, 'UD: Delelinjeavtalen inneholder ingen klausul om oppsigelse' ['Ministry of Foreign Affairs: The Delimitation Agreement Contains No Clause On Termination'], 5 July 2022, <https://www.nrk.no/nyheter/ud_---delelinjeavtalen-inneholder-ingen-klausul-om-oppsigelse-1.16028229>, accessed 30 April 2023.

influential towards Oslo, followed by – or reinforced with – military power projection.[13] Therefore, Russia's diplomatic signalling must also be seen in conjunction with the other instruments of Russian power, such as its 'information confrontations' and military force demonstrations.

Information and Disinformation: Conflicting Narratives

As part of Russia's whole-of-government approach to its foreign and security policy objectives, its diplomatic efforts are regularly supported by information and cyber operations to reinforce the Russian narrative, while sowing doubts about – or discrediting – the competing narrative.[14] Such 'weaponisation of information' is within the domain of 'information confrontation', a uniquely Russian term that includes information and cyber operations.[15]

In 2022, all three Norwegian security services (the Norwegian Intelligence Service (NIS), the Police Security Service (PST), and the National Security Authority (NSM)) renewed their warnings of there being a high and persistent threat posed by Russian state and non-state actors in spreading disinformation and conducting cyber operations.[16] According to the three services, Russian state or state-affiliated actors are the most severe threats to Norwegian domestic security interests and actively attempt to influence the government's decision-making processes, limit strategic options and weaken Norwegian national security interests.[17]

According to the Norwegian Defence Research Establishment (FFI), Norway is likely not among Russia's most prioritised targets. However, there is a persistent effort by Russia's GRU (foreign military intelligence) and SVR (foreign intelligence service) in Norway.[18] Their general objectives are likely 'to weaken Western democracies through increased polarization, weakening public confidence in the government, and undermining and manipulating the perception of reality to both its own and other countries' populations'.[19] It is also likely that their specific objectives towards Norway are to 'influence attitudes in the Norwegian population and Norway's position in international politics' due to its geostrategic location, in combination with it being a NATO member.[20] Furthermore, the FFI report states that 'Russian authorities and personnel at the Russian Embassy in Oslo are active, both through diplomacy, intelligence, lobbying, and editorial and social media activity'.[21] Recently, on 13 April 2023, Norwegian authorities expelled 15 persons employed at the Russian Embassy in Oslo on the grounds that 'their activities are a threat to Norwegian interests' according to the Minister of Foreign Affairs, Anniken Huitfeldt.[22]

Russian information operations are often based on official statements to the Russian and international media, at times reinforced by ambiguous

13. Norwegian Intelligence Service (NIS), 'Fokus 2022' ['Focus 2022'], 11 February 2022, p. 39, <https://www.forsvaret.no/aktuelt-og-presse/publikasjoner/fokus>, accessed 29 April 2023.
14. Antony J Blinken, 'Taking Action to Expose and Disrupt Russia's Destabilisation Campaign in Ukraine', US Department of State, 20 January 2022, <https://www.state.gov/taking-action-to-expose-and-disrupt-russias-destabilization-campaign-in-ukraine>, accessed 18 February 2022.
15. NIS, 'Fokus 2022', p. 34.
16. *Ibid.*, p. 8; Police Security Service (PST), 'Nasjonal trusselvurdering 2022' ['National Threat Assessment 2022'], 24 January 2022, pp. 8–14, <https://pst.no/globalassets/ntv/2022/nasjonal-trusselvurdering-2022-pa-norsk.pdf?msclkid=04b03b8ea69c11ec85d819862a3979ac>, accessed 3 August 2022; National Security Authority (NSM), 'Risiko 2022' ['Risk 2022'], 11 February 2022, p. 17, <https://nsm.no/getfile.php/137798-1644424185/NSM/Filer/Dokumenter/Rapporter/NSM_rapport_final_online_enekeltsider.pdf>, accessed 29 April 2023.
17. PST, 'Nasjonal trusselvurdering', pp. 8–14, and NSM, 'Risiko 2022', p. 17.
18. Eskil Grendahl Sivertsen et al., 'Hvordan gjøre samfunnet mer robust mot uønsket påvirkning i sosiale medier' ['How to Make Society More Resilient Against Unwanted Social Media Influences'], in FFI-report 21/01237, Norwegian Defence Research Establishment (FFI), 9 June 2021, p. 31, <https://www.ffi.no/publikasjoner/arkiv/hvordan-gjore-samfunnet-mer-robust-mot-uonsket-pavirkning-i-sosiale-medier>, accessed 28 April 2023.
19. *Ibid.*
20. *Ibid.*
21. *Ibid.*
22. Tonje Grimstad et al., 'Ansatte ved Russlands ambassade sendes ut fra Norge: – En trussel mot Norge', ['Employees of the Russian Embassy are being Expelled From Norway: 'A Threat to Norway'], *NRK*, 13 April 2023, <https://www.nrk.no/norge/ansatte-ved-russlands-ambassade-utvises-fra-norge_-_-en-trussel-mot-norge-1.16372116>, accessed 30 April 2023.

or unattributable sources spreading disinformation via social media and other decentralised platforms.[23] While Russian official statements may provide consistent – although alternative – narratives, other unattributable sources are to a greater degree used for spreading disinformation and conflicting narratives aimed at exploiting perceived vulnerabilities in democratic societies by attempting to exacerbate divisions, thereby seeking to degrade societal cohesion.[24]

A consistent trend in Moscow's official statements is that the Norwegian government is manipulating public opinion related to Russo-Norwegian bilateral relations. Ministry of Foreign Affairs (MFA) spokesperson Maria Zakharova goes as far as claiming that 'Norwegians are being misled [by] Oslo'.[25] Also, Moscow has occasionally attempted to exploit perceived divisions in Norway through statements such as 'Oslo is ignorant of the security of "northerners"' by allowing US submarines to enter its northern ports. Although Moscow is failing to gain traction in its information campaign, it clearly shows that Moscow pays attention to Norwegian politics to identify areas where it can inflame societal divisions.[26]

In another case of 'weaponisation of disinformation', Russia has resorted to falsifying Automatic Identification System (AIS) location data.[27] One such incident involved Royal Norwegian Navy (RNoN) vessels operating in the Baltic Sea on 14 June 2020. According to publicly available Marine Traffic AIS data, the two RNoN corvettes operating in the region falsely appeared to have violated Russian territorial waters outside the Kaliningrad enclave as a consequence of AIS receiver stations being fed falsified location data by non-attributable cyber-actors.[28] Although this incident did not involve actual ships emitting the false location data, other incidents did. According to information disclosed through the Norwegian Freedom of Information Act, the RNoN points to Russia as a likely source of such disinformation in at least one specific case in September 2020, where two Russian warships operating between Norway and Denmark emitted AIS signals identifying them as Norwegian and Danish frigates.[29]

Norwegian Department of Defence spokespersons stated that an adversary may have multiple purposes for falsifying location data. The manipulation of location information is seen as a broadening of ongoing disinformation campaigns in social media and the press aimed at undermining the credibility and reliability of governments and institutions in the West. Furthermore, in case of a confrontation at sea, falsified information may be used to substantiate false claims or to support allegations of violations of sovereign states' territorial waters, thereby adding to the Russian narrative that it is surrounded by aggressors.[30] Another aspect is that the demonstration of such capacities and capabilities is likely to support Russia's wider strategic deterrence signalling. In another noteworthy event, Putin signed the Russian Federation's 2022 Maritime Doctrine on 31 July 2022. This doctrine places an increased emphasis on employing civilian vessels for military purposes, potentially further blurring the lines between combatants and non-combatants at sea.[31]

23. Lesley Kucharski, 'Russian Multi-Domain Strategy Against NATO: Information Confrontation and U.S. Forward-deployed Nuclear Weapons in Europe', Lawrence Livermore National Laboratory: Center for Global Security Research, pp. 2–3.
24. *Ibid.*
25. Atle Staalesen, 'Moscow Lashes Out Against Oslo, But Courts Norwegian Population', *Barents Observer*, 23 November 2020, <https://thebarentsobserver.com/en/security/2020/11/moscow-lashes-out-against-oslo-courts-norwegian-population>, accessed 23 February 2023.
26. The Russian Embassy in Oslo, 'Om anløp av amerikanske atomubåter til Tønsneshavn ved Tromsø'.
27. Henrik Lied, 'Norske marineskip ble manipulert inn i russisk farvann' ['Norwegian Warships Manipulated into Russian Waters'], *NRK Beta*, 25 September 2021, <https://nrkbeta.no/2021/09/25/norske-marineskip-ble-manipulert-inn-i-russisk-farvann>, accessed 29 April 2023.
28. *Ibid.*
29. *NRK Beta*, 'Innsyn Falsk AIS', ['Access to Information on False AIS'], September 2021, <http://nrkbeta.no/wp-content/uploads/2021/09/innsyn_falsk_ais.pdf>, accessed 28 April 2023.
30. *Ibid.*
31. President of the Russian Federation, 'Ukaz Prezidenta Rossijskoj Federacii ot 31.07.2022 # 512 "Ob utverzhdenii Morskoj doktriny Rossijskoj Federacii"' ['Decree No. 512 of the President of the Russian Federation, 31 July 2022, On the Approval of the Maritime Doctrine of the Russian Federation'], pp. 2–10, <http://publication.pravo.gov.ru/Document/View/0001202207310001>, accessed 31 July 2022.

Another trend is Russia's continuous effort to export its 'memorial diplomacy' to Norway.[32] In particular, this can be seen through the continued emphasis on constructing and maintaining public memorial sites in the north-eastern region of Finnmark, which was liberated from German occupation in 1944 by the Soviet Red Army. Commentators suggest that this is part of a broader strategy by Russia to cultivate a sense of gratitude and obligation from the Norwegian side.[33] This approach may also seek to divert attention from negative publicity and reinforce a positive image of Russia.

The overall effects sought by Moscow in its information operations are likely two-fold. On the one hand, it aims to construct a narrative through official statements or Russian and Norwegian media that Oslo is ignoring Russia's interests and misleading its population by offering its territory to NATO as a springboard from which to threaten Russia's security interests. On the other hand, this feeds into a domestic narrative in Russia, where Norway and NATO are portrayed as aggressive and encroaching on Russian sovereignty. Taken together, Russia's signalling could be considered an active information campaign and is likely aimed at undermining public trust in the Norwegian government and influencing government decision-making.

According to NSM, cyber attacks causing serious consequences tripled from 2019 to 2021.[34] Although most were of criminal character, some also targeted Norwegian national security interests. These attacks target academic or government institutions and companies possessing advanced manufacturing technologies. NSM claims that the attacks aim to gain insight into government policymaking and to access otherwise inaccessible technology.[35] The majority of such attacks remain either unattributable or are otherwise ambiguous. This is further complicated by the fact that several attacks are attributed to third-party actors, thereby creating sufficient ambiguity to remain plausibly deniable by their suspected sponsor. It is also likely that some state or state-sponsored cyber attacks have remained undiscovered due to the increasingly sophisticated means and ways of such activities.[36]

However, in late 2014, an advanced network of false GSM transceiver stations was discovered in the vicinity of the parliament and government administration buildings in Oslo and is assumed to have been monitoring government officials.[37] The system's sophistication indicated that foreign state actors were involved, but the incident was not publicly attributed. In 2020, the Norwegian parliament's email system came under attack from what the PST and NSM attributed to the 'Fancy Bear' (APT-28) cyber espionage group affiliated with GRU.[38] In a historic move, the Norwegian MFA publicly attributed the incident to Russia, calling it an unacceptable attack on Norway's democratic interests.[39] In 2022, the University of Tromsø was subjected to a cyber attack in which the attackers targeted the email accounts of security policy researchers; a PST investigation later attributed the

32. The Russian Embassy in Oslo, 'Om avdukningen av minnesmerket over sovjetiske flygere I Norge' ['About the Unveiling of the Memorial to Soviet Pilots in Norway'], 7 October 2021, <https://norway.mid.ru/no/embassy/press-centre/news/om_avduking_av_minnesmerket_over_sovjetiske_flygere_i_norge/>, accessed 17 February 2023.
33. Jade McGlynn, 'Moscow is Using Memory Diplomacy to Export its Narrative to the World', *Foreign Policy*, 25 June 2021; Allan Klo, 'Tror Russland bruker krigsminnesmerker for å påvirke nordmenn' ['Believe Russia is Using War Memorials to Influence Norwegians'], *NRK*, 31 October 2021, <https://www.nrk.no/tromsogfinnmark/hedda-langemyr-tror-russland-bruker-krigsminnesmerker-for-a-pavirke-nordmenn-1.15708160?msclkid=da94c830a57411ec86782cb5ef63c6fd>, accessed 29 April 2023.
34. NSM, 'Risiko 2022', p. 26.
35. *Ibid*., pp. 7–14.
36. *Ibid*., p. 19.
37. Norwegian Parliament, 'Innstilling fra justiskomiteen om redegjørelse av justis- og beredskapsministeren om falske basestasjoner' ['Recommendation from the Justice Committee on the Account of the Minister of Justice and Public Security about False Transceiver Stations'], 5 May 2015, <https://www.stortinget.no/no/Saker-og-publikasjoner/Publikasjoner/Referater/Stortinget/2014-2015/150505/10/?msclkid=b1889dc5a57311eca10a02fca3fb959f>, accessed 17 March 2022.
38. Jan M Olsen, 'Norway Intel: Russians Likely Behind Parliament Hacking', *Associated Press*, 8 December 2020, <https://apnews.com/article/denmark-europe-military-intelligence-hacking-norway-fd69246508dc8621821afab5d0eace09>, accessed 15 March 2022.
39. Marius H Larsen, 'Regjeringen beskylder Russland for datainnbrudd på Stortinget' ['The Government Accuses Russia of Hacking into the Norwegian Parliament's Computer Network'], *Forsvarets Forum*, 13 October 2020, <https://forsvaretsforum.no/cyber-russland/regjeringen-beskylder-russland-for-datainnbrudd-pa-stortinget/165142>, accessed 29 April 2023.

attack to Russia.[40] Later the same year, a 'Brazilian' researcher was arrested at Tromsø university and charged with espionage. According to the PST, the researcher's real identity was that of a Russian national.[41] Open-source investigator Christo Grozev at Bellingcat, however, claims that the person is a GRU colonel.[42]

Another factor of note is Russia's covert or overt attempts to gain access to advanced technology. While covert attempts are in the realm of industrial espionage, overt efforts involve attempted purchases of products or companies.[43] According to the NIS and PST, there is a particular demand for Norwegian maritime and other advanced technology. This was exemplified by the Russian Trans Mash Holding's attempt to buy the Rolls Royce Group subsidiary Bergen Engines in 2021.[44] The Norwegian government prohibited the sale based on concerns that the company had strong ties to Russian authorities. It is believed that the acquisition of Bergen Engines, which specialises in manufacturing large ship engines for customers such as the Norwegian and US navies, would once again enable the construction of larger Russian naval vessels after losing access to such engines following its 2014 invasion of Crimea.[45]

Overall, Russian activity in the information and cyber domains appears to be part of a comprehensive approach, which includes disinformation and espionage, aimed at influencing government decision-making, undermining democratic processes, and acquiring otherwise inaccessible information and technology.

Military: Combining Old Concepts with New Approaches

Despite Moscow's stated ambition of keeping tensions low in the Arctic, there are several examples of ways in which the Russian military is being used to signal disagreements with Oslo, especially since the 2014 degradation of political relations.

In 2015, Russia's deputy prime minister, Dmitry Rogozin, made an unannounced visit to Longyearbyen in Svalbard despite being on Norway's 2014 sanctions list of persons prohibited from entering the country.[46] Furthermore, Chechen special forces affiliated with the Russian FSB's Alpha group made a stopover in Longyearbyen in 2016, allegedly on their way to an exercise near the North Pole.[47] Norwegian Svalbard policy clearly states that 'all foreign military activity in Svalbard is prohibited and would entail a gross infringement of Norway's sovereignty'.[48] Such actions are highly problematic and pose severe challenges to the 1920 Svalbard Treaty by exploiting the grey zone in the treaty's definition of 'military activity'.

40. Øyvind B Skille, 'Russland skal stå bak dataangrep mot nordområde-forskere' ['Russia Behind Computer Attacks Against Security Policy Researchers'], *NRK*, 28 February 2022, <https://www.nrk.no/tromsogfinnmark/russland-skal-sta-bak-dataangrep-mot-nordomrade-forskere-i-tromso-1.15872979?msclkid=830e3811a58911ec9fa4a93a3a850ca1>, accessed 17 March 2022.
41. Anne Skifjeld et al., 'PST sikter spionmistenkt i Tromsø: Mener de har hans russiske identitet' ['PST Charges Spy Suspect in Tromsø'], *NRK*, 28 October 2022, <https://www.nrk.no/norge/pst-sikter-spionmistenkt-i-tromso_-mener-de-har-hans-russiske-identitet-1.16156368>, accessed 27 February 2023.
42. @christogrozev, 'Bingo! He was registered at the address of the dormitory of the GRU academy. Which means he's no less than a colonel! Great job, Norway - you've caught yourself a colonel from the GRU', Twitter post, 28 October 2022, <https://twitter.com/christogrozev/status/1585999431966625794>, accessed 22 February 2023.
43. PST, 'Nasjonal trusselvurdering 2022', p. 10.
44. NIS, 'Fokus 2022', p. 21.
45. *Ibid.*
46. Thomas Nilsen, 'Russian Defence Report Lists Norway's Svalbard Policy as Potential Risk of War', *Arctic Today*, 4 October 2017, <https://www.arctictoday.com/russia-defense-report-lists-norways-svalbard-policy-as-potential-risk-of-war/>, accessed 14 March 2022; Norwegian Ministry of Foreign Affairs, 'Forskrift om restriktive tiltak mot personer som anses ansvarlige for underslag av offentlige midler, samt personer som anses å ha deltatt i menneskerettighetsbrudd i Ukraina' ['Regulations Relating to Restrictive Measures against Persons Deemed Responsible for Embezzlement of Public Funds, as well as Persons Deemed to have Participated in Human Rights Violations in Ukraine'], 9 May 2014, <https://lovdata.no/dokument/SF/forskrift/2014-05-09-612?q=ukraina>, accessed 7 February 2022.
47. Trude Pettersen, 'Chechen Special Forces Instructors Landed on Svalbard', *Barents Observer*, 13 April 2016, <https://thebarentsobserver.com/en/2016/04/chechen-special-forces-instructors-landed-svalbard>, accessed 3 March 2022.
48. Norwegian Government, 'Meld. St. 32 (2015-2016) Svalbard' ['Government Report no. 32 to the Parliament (2015-2016) Svalbard'], 11 May 2016, p. 21, <https://www.regjeringen.no/no/dokumenter/meld.-st.-32-20152016/id2499962/>, accessed 27 February 2023.

In 2017, a Russian defence report on threats to its national interests identified Norway as a specific threat by what the report described as Norway's 'unilateral revision of international agreements', likely in reference to the Svalbard Treaty, and its move 'towards establishing absolute national jurisdiction over Spitsbergen [Svalbard] and the adjacent 200 nautical mile boundary around it'.[49] Additionally, Russian state-affiliated media outlets openly questioned the legitimacy of Norway's claim to the archipelago, clearly seeking to inflame a revisionist debate.[50]

According to the treaty, Svalbard is not to be used for 'war-like purposes'. Therefore, Norwegian military use of Svalbard is limited to essential and non-permanent activities (including Coast Guard visits and military aircraft conducting civil transportation and search-and-rescue operations).[51] Since the mid-2000s, there has also been an annual visit by an RNoN frigate to the archipelago. This routinely draws criticism from Moscow; however, Russia's 2021 MFA statement was particularly explicit:

> [Oslo's] next step in [...] a series of consistent actions to include this territory in the sphere of national military construction [...] which implies the use of the archipelago's infrastructure in the military planning of Norway's defence, including the reception of reinforcements from NATO allies. Coupled with the SvalSat satellite ground tracking station operating in the archipelago, technically equipped to perform dual-use tasks, the practice of using the [Longyearbyen] airport by Norwegian military transport aircraft, patrolling the Svalbard waters by Coast Guard ships – all these facts indicate an increase in the tendency of covert militarization of the archipelago by the Norwegian side'.[52]

Interestingly, the 2021 RNoN visit to Svalbard was followed by what appears to be a response by the Northern Fleet (NFLT). Although the NFLT has conducted annual 'Arctic voyages' for the past decade, the 2021 voyage deviated from previous years when the destroyer *Severomorsk* and two support vessels set course for the waters around Svalbard. The NFLT stated that the ships were sent to carry out 'a set of measures aimed at protecting the interests of the Russian Federation in the Arctic'.[53] According to a Norwegian Joint Headquarters spokesperson, such behaviour had not been seen before.[54] Although the NFLT's land component has suffered severe losses in Ukraine, its air and maritime component continues to create a considerable regional asymmetry.

The Russian air force is also being used to relay Moscow's dissatisfaction with Norwegian policy and has conducted several simulated strikes on Norwegian installations and vessels in recent years. In a 2018 speech, the former Chief of the NIS, Morten Haga Lunde, disclosed that Russia conducted three separate simulated airstrikes on Norwegian facilities and vessels in 2017.[55] According to Lunde, the coercive air campaign began with nine aircraft conducting repeated simulated strikes on the NIS's GLOBUS II radar in Vardø (Norway's easternmost point). The incident was likely intended to signal Moscow's discontent and frustration over the ongoing construction of the US-funded GLOBUS

49. Alexandra Djordjevic, Ivan Safronov and Dmitriy Kozlov, 'Geopolitika v pomoshh' snabzheniju', ['Geopolitics to Help Supply'], *Kommersant*, 3 October 2017, <https://www.kommersant.ru/doc/3428044>, accessed 29 April 2023.
50. Alexander Khrolenko, 'NATO Gets All Hot and Bothered for Norwegian Archipelago, Russia Says Stay Out', *Sputnik News*, 20 April 2017, <https://sputniknews.com/politics/201704201052827663-norway-russia-nato-archipelago-dispute/>, accessed 14 March 2022.
51. Norwegian Government, 'St. Meld. 22 (2008-2009) Svalbard', [Government Report No. 22 to the Parliament (2008-2009) Svalbard], 17 April 2009, p. 23, <https://www.regjeringen.no/no/dokumenter/stmeld-nr-22-2008-2009-/id554877/>, accessed 12 May 2023.
52. Russia's Ministry of Foreign Affairs, 'Kommentarij oficial'nogo predstavitelja MID Rossii M.V.Zaharovoj v svjazi s norvezhskoj voennoj aktivnost'ju na arhipelage Shpicbergen', ['Comment by MFA Spokesperson Maria Zakharova on Norwegian Military Activity in the Spitsbergen Archipelago'], 12 November 2021, <https://archive.mid.ru/ru/foreign_policy/news/-/asset_publisher/cKNonkJE02Bw/content/id/4934485>, accessed 29 April 2023.
53. Thomas Nilsen, 'In a Surprise Direction NFLT Grouping Sails West of Svalbard on Annual Arctic Voyage', *Barents Observer*, 18 August 2021, <https://thebarentsobserver.com/en/security/2021/08/surprise-direction-northern-fleet-grouping-sails-west-svalbard-annual-arctic-voyage>, accessed 14 March 2022.
54. *Ibid*.
55. Thomas Nilsen, 'Russian Bombers Simulated an Attack against this Radar on Norway's Barents Sea Coast', *Barents Observer*, 5 March 2018, <https://thebarentsobserver.com/en/security/2018/03/russian-bombers-simulated-attack-against-radar-norways-barents-sea-coast>, accessed 6 January 2023.

III radar on the site by 2022, suspecting that the radar would be part of a US early warning system.[56]

Two months later, 12 Russian aircraft simulated a strike on a maritime group consisting of naval vessels from Norway and other NATO member states, while participating in the anti-submarine Exercise EASTLANT in the northern part of the Norwegian Sea. According to Lunde, the Russian force consisted of MiG-31 interceptors, SU-24 multi-role aircraft and Tu-22M long-range strategic bombers.[57] Exercise EASTLANT was also countered by an NFLT naval response, as is customary when NATO forces operate in the northern Norwegian Sea or the Barents Sea. The week after, nine Russian aircraft simulated strikes on the Norwegian Air Force's air station in Bodø. The simulated attack took place during the *Arctic Challenge* Exercise, which involved fighter aircraft from several allied countries.[58]

Although Russian air force activity is routinely intercepted by Norwegian fighter aircraft on NATO Quick Reaction Alert (QRA), the actions described by Lunde were of a character that required a sharp response from the Norwegian authorities, stating that such behaviour is contributing to 'a decline in confidence, predictability, and stability in the North'.[59] Nevertheless, in early 2018, 11 Su-24 aircraft repeated their simulated strikes on the GLOBUS II radar (see Figure 1).[60]

Another emerging trend is the NFLT's excessive use of maritime danger areas, referred to in Russian as 'PRIPs' (also commonly referred to as Notice to Airmen – NOTAMs).[61] As these areas are used for anything from small-arms to submarine launched ballistic missile tests, they effectively become maritime exclusion zones. By the end of 2022, the Russian Western Arctic Sea Port Administration had issued 59 PRIPs, compared with 31 for 2021 and 11 in 2020.[62] Military danger areas are usually intended to ensure the safety of the issuing authority and those who would otherwise have ventured into the given areas. However, there are indications that PRIPs are used both as a political signalling tool and as a military means for peacetime sea denial. As a political tool, PRIPs have been used to signal dissatisfaction with Norwegian and allied activity in the High North, such as during the NATO exercise *Trident Juncture* in 2018 and other exercises where Russia has announced disruptive PRIPs within the Alliance's declared exercise areas.[63] Russian PRIPs are also used as a military means in ways that serve its security strategy by creating temporary 'geo-fences' to block or canalise military activity away from areas or activities considered to be sensitive to Russia, such as by obstructing access to the Barents Sea or to observe weapons tests. Since 2014, Russia has also announced numerous PRIPs inside Norway's exclusive economic zone without apparent military necessity.[64] This practice also parallels Russian conduct in the waters and airspace around occupied Crimea.[65]

PRIPs are also a source of economic loss for those who would otherwise use the sea for civil purposes, such as seasonal fisheries, commerce, air traffic to and from oil and gas platforms, and occasionally to the operation of the platforms themselves.[66] While the practice adheres to international law and conforms to international

56. *Ibid*.; NIS, 'Oppgradering av GLOBUS-systemet' ['Upgrading the GLOBUS system'], 10 June 2022, <https://www.etterretningstjenesten.no/aktuelt/aktuelt/oppgradering-av-globus-systemet?q=Globus>, accessed 29 April 2023.
57. Nilsen, 'Russian Bombers Simulated an Attack against this Radar on Norway's Barents Sea Coast'.
58. *Ibid*.
59. *Ibid*.
60. Thomas Nilsen, '11 Russian Fighter Jets Made Mock Attack on Norwegian Arctic Radar', *Barents Observer*, 12 February 2019, <https://thebarentsobserver.com/en/security/2019/02/11-russian-fighter-jets-made-mock-attack-norwegian-arctic-radar>, accessed 14 March 2022.
61. National Geospatial-Intelligence Agency, 'Pub. 180 Sailing Directions Arctic Ocean', 2020, p. 177, <https://msi.nga.mil/api/publications/download?type=view&key=16694492/SFH00000/Pub180bk.pdf>, accessed 28 April 2023.
62. Western Arctic Sea Ports Authority, 'PRIP Murmansk', <http://www.mapm.ru/Prip>, accessed 2 January 2023.
63. Jack Watling, 'NATO's Trident Juncture 2018 Exercise: Political Theatre with a Purpose', *RUSI Commentary*, 20 November 2018.
64. Kristian Åtland, Thomas Nilsen and Torbjørn Pedersen, 'Military Muscle-Flexing as Interstate Communication: Russian NOTAM Warnings off the Coast of Norway, 2015–2021', *Scandinavian Journal of Military Studies* (Vol. 5, No. 1, 2022), pp. 63–78.
65. *UAWire*, 'Russia Closes Airspace over Crimea and Parts of Black Sea', 20 April 2021, <https://uawire.org/russia-closes-airspace-over-crimea-and-black-sea>, accessed 30 April 2023.
66. Thomas Nilsen, 'Russia Issues the Largest-ever Warning Zone in the Norwegian Part of the Barents Sea', *Barents Observer*, 15 February 2022, <https://thebarentsobserver.com/en/security/2022/02/largest-ever-russian-notam-warning-norwegian-sector-barents-sea>, accessed 26 February 2022.

Figure 1: Flight Patterns of 11 Su-24s Conducting Repeated Simulated Strikes on GLOBUS II in 2018

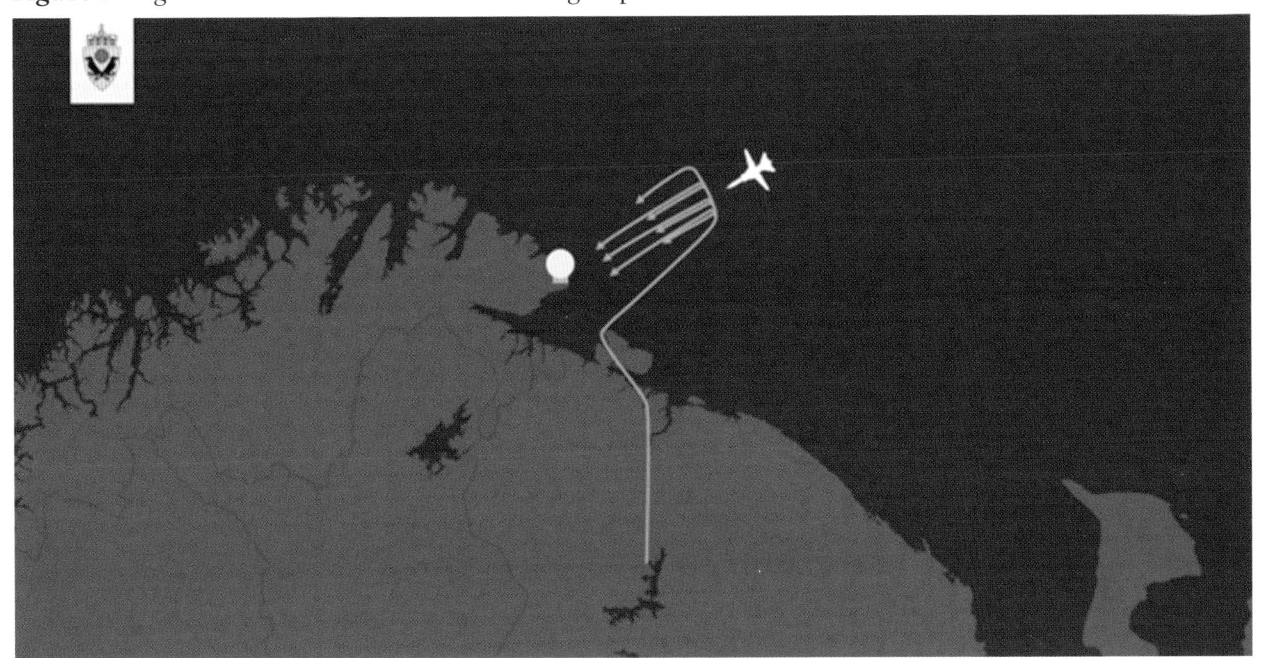

Source: The Norwegian Intelligence Service.

notification requirements, it demonstrates a lack of regard for economic activities and regularly results in complaints from Norwegian fishery organisations claiming that the practice is violating Norway's sovereign rights.[67]

On 19 February 2022, Russia activated the most comprehensive PRIPs since the Cold War, in conjunction with executing its delayed Grom (Thunder) strategic nuclear deterrence exercise.[68] The PRIPs effectively closed off much of the ice-free parts of the Barents Sea, including large parts of Norway's economic zone in the region. The PRIPs and the activity within them likely served several national security strategy ends. The exercise demonstrated the viability of Russia's strategic nuclear deterrence assets, willingness to protect its national interests in the region by ensuring freedom of action and movement, and demonstrating Russian regional military hegemony. In relation to Norway, the exercise signalled a policy change by launching a nuclear-capable 3M22 Zircon hypersonic missile from inside Norway's economic zone around Bjørnøya (Bear Island). But, more importantly, the exercise demonstrated resolve and the viability of its nuclear deterrence triad only days before its second invasion of Ukraine.

In other maritime incidents, Russian trawlers have been suspected of being involved in damaging vital seabed infrastructure. On 3 April 2021, the Lofoten Vesterålen (LoVe) underwater monitoring cable stopped working. The cable was a joint scientific venture between the Norwegian Institute of Marine Research (Havforskningsinstituttet) and the FFI, intended to monitor maritime acoustic activity. Investigations showed that 4.3 km of cable had disappeared from a location 3 km outside of Norwegian territorial waters and was later recovered 11 km from its original position. The subsequent police investigation concluded that several Russian trawlers had been engaged in trawling at the location and time in question, however, the case was later dropped.[69]

In another cable incident, one of the two communication cables between Svalbard and mainland Norway ceased to operate on 7 January 2022. The police investigation found that several of

67. *Ibid.*; Bård Wormdal, 'Fiskere fortviler over russisk storøvelse' ['Fishermen Despair Over Russian Exercise'], *NRK*, 15 February 2022, <https://www.nrk.no/tromsogfinnmark/havfiskeflaten-reagerer-pa-russisk-storovelse-_-fiskebat-mener-ovelsen-er-en-overkjoring-av-norge-1.15855910>, accessed 25 February 2022.

68. The Kremlin, 'Uchenie sil strategicheskogo sderzhivanija' ['Strategic Deterrence Exercise'], 19 February 2022, <http://www.kremlin.ru/events/president/news/67814>, accessed 25 February 2022.

69. Benjamin Fredriksen, 'Kabelmysteriet' ['The Cable Mysteries'], *NRK*, 26 June 2022, <https://www.nrk.no/nordland/xl/russiske-tralere-krysset-kabler-i-vesteralen-og-svalbard-for-brudd-1.16007084>, accessed 2 January 2023.

the same trawlers as in the previous incident were present in the area, but again, the case was dropped. Space Norway owns and operates the cable which serves as the primary communication line for the population on Svalbard and the Norwegian mainland.[70]

Although neither of the two cable incidents could be attributed to Russian state involvement, they show the vulnerability of seabed infrastructure, even to relatively simple interference. According to a 2018 study by the Centre for Strategic and International Studies (CSIS), Russia has the world's most developed force for seabed warfare, organised around its Main Directorate for Deep-Sea Research, capable of a wide array of missions, including tapping or severing undersea cables.[71] According to the study, the Directorate interfered with the 2015 completion of the SweLit undersea power cable in the Baltic Sea, proving its capability and willingness to influence undersea infrastructure.[72] Considering Norway's extensive reliance on undersea infrastructure, especially in the offshore oil and gas sector, such disruptive warfare may represent a severe challenge to Norwegian and European interests, as seen in the 2022 Nord Stream incident where unidentified actors sabotaged the pipelines, rendering them inoperable.

Furthermore, Russia routinely disrupts Global Navigation Satellite System (GNSS) receivers in northern Norway as a means of political and military signalling. Such actions occur regularly and represent a severe problem by degrading the accuracy of the country's position, navigation and time (PNT) dependent sectors.[73] Conducting electronic warfare (EW) in peacetime may have catastrophic effects on PNT-dependent platforms, such as aircraft or ships.

The GNSS disruptions initially occurred most frequently from 2017 through the 2018 NATO exercise *Trident Juncture* and well into 2019. Despite voicing formal complaints to Russian authorities, the EW activity continued and compelled the Norwegian Department of Transportation to gather 'undisputable evidence', which concluded that the signal emitters were located on the Kola peninsula.[74] Despite objections from the Norwegian MFA, Russia did not end the disruptive and coercive behaviour. Russia only ceased its GNSS disruption operations six months later, following further bilateral talks in June 2019.[75]

In the incident report on the 2017–2019 GNSS disruptions, the Norwegian Justice Department concluded that the loss of GNSS signals would affect the overall ability to effectively manage civil crisis response preparedness in northern Norway.[76] From a military perspective, such low-cost EW can also degrade the effectiveness of high-tech precision-guided munitions (PGM) depending on GPS signals, reducing the overall deterrence effect of the Norwegian or NATO PGM inventory.[77] The incidents also show the impact and cost such strategic signalling has across several sectors of Norwegian society, as it demanded a coordinated response from the Ministry of Transport, the Ministry of Defense and the Ministry of Foreign Affairs. In 2022–2023, the EW activity resumed, increasing five-fold compared with 2017–2020, again causing problems for air traffic.[78]

70. Alf R Jacobsen, 'Kabelbruddet til Svalbardmysteriet løst' ['The Cable Break to Svalbard: Mystery Solved?'], 16 February 2022, <www.document.no/2022/02/16/kabelbruddet-til-svalbard-mysteriet-lost>, accessed 9 March 2022.
71. Andrew Metrick and Kathleen H Hicks, 'Contested Seas: Maritime Domain Awareness in Northern Europe', CSIS, 2018, p. 7; H I Sutton, '5 Ways the Russian Navy Could Target Undersea Internet Cables', *Naval News*, 7 April 2021, <https://www.navalnews.com/naval-news/2021/04/5-ways-the-russian-navy-could-target-undersea-internet-cables/>, accessed 11 March 2022.
72. *Ibid.*
73. Norwegian Ministry of Transport, 'Rapport fra arbeidsgruppen GNSS/ GPS-forstyrrelser innen luftfart' ['Report From the Working Group On GNSS/GPS Interference in Aviation'], 19 December 2019, p. 3, <https://www.regjeringen.no/no/dokumenter/forstyrrelser-innen-luftfart/id2789626/>, accessed 28 April 2023.
74. *Ibid.*, p. 6.
75. *Ibid.*
76. *Ibid.*, p. 13.
77. Roger N McDermott, *Russia's Electronic Warfare Capabilities to 2025: Challenging NATO in the Electromagnetic Spectrum* (Tallinn: International Centre for Defence and Security, 2017), p. 14.
78. Stian Strøm, 'Kraftig økning av GPS-jamming over Finnmark' ['Sharp Increase in Jamming Over Finnmark'], *NRK*, 24 February 2023, <https://www.nrk.no/tromsogfinnmark/kraftig-okning-av-gps-jamming-over-finnmark-1.16309499>, accessed 25 February 2023.

Figure 2: Russian PNT Jamming During *Trident Juncture* 2018

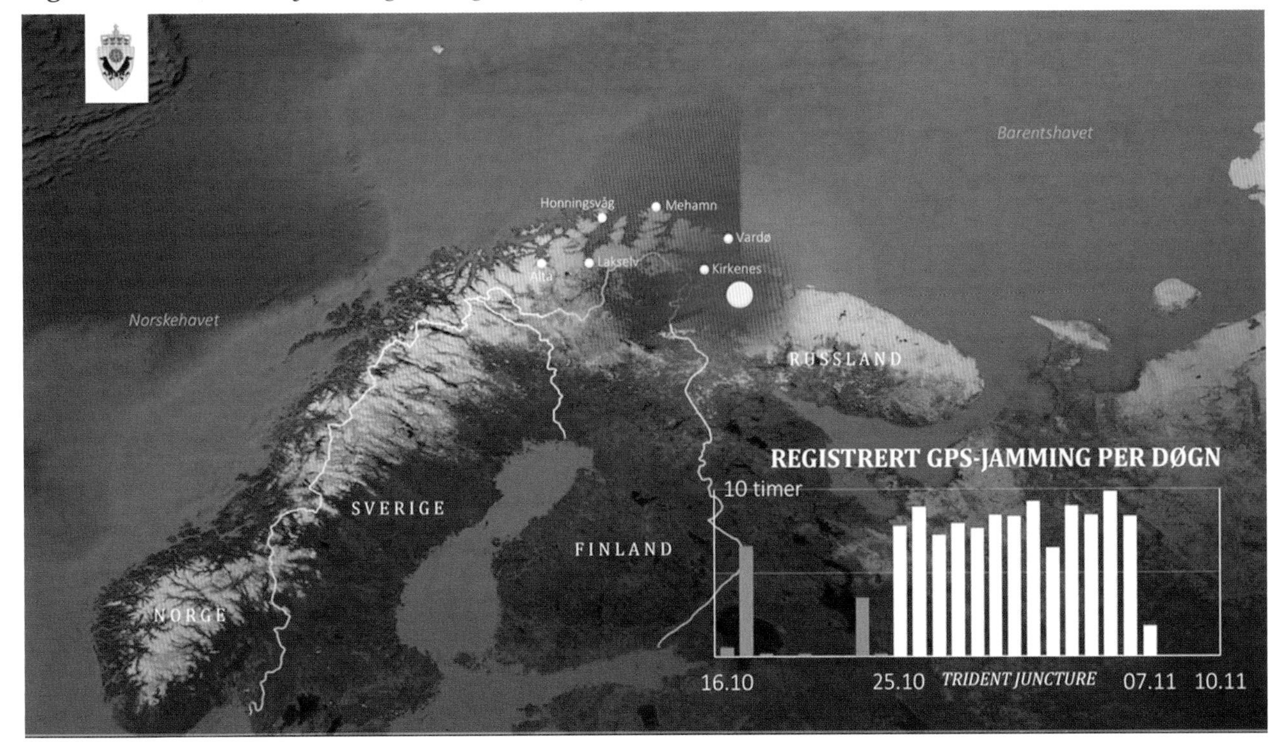

Source: The Norwegian Intelligence Service.

Russia: A Challenge to Norwegian Interests and Options?

Overall, when considering Russia's coercive campaign in the diplomatic, information and military domains in the timeframe 2014–2023, it is clear that Moscow's security policy objectives are related to the Svalbard archipelago, US and NATO forces operating on or out of the Norwegian mainland, and opposition to the 2014 and 2022 sanctions policy. It is also clear that Russia seeks to gain access to otherwise inaccessible security policy related information and advanced technology.

As described, these objectives are pursued through covert, ambiguous or openly coercive sub-threshold activities, and range from official statements, disinformation campaigns, and espionage, to hacking, cyber attacks and military force demonstrations, with the aim of gaining access to government or corporate information, influencing decision-making, and compelling Oslo to comply with its foreign and security policy objectives. However, these activities have been somewhat irregular in both time and intensity.

Russia's sub-threshold activities towards Norway may be viewed from two different perspectives. On the one hand, they could be seen as evidence of a confident Russia seeking to assert its influence and achieve its objectives by any means necessary. On the other hand, the activities may also be considered as acts of desperation, resulting from a failure to achieve its goals through cooperative and peaceful means. Regardless of the perspective taken, it is clear that Russia's efforts have succeeded in degrading the relationship between the two nations.

Whether or not Moscow has achieved any of its desired outcomes, its increased risk acceptance and violations of the international rules-based order have created the impression that the Russian bear is wounded, which makes it more dangerous and unpredictable than ever before. ■

Runar Spansvoll is a Commander (OF3) in the Norwegian Armed Forces. Unless otherwise stated, the views presented in this article are solely those of the author and do not represent those of institutions or organisations with which the author is associated.

This article is based on a dissertation submitted to the Department of War Studies, School of Social Science and Public Policy at King's College London.

Military History

Deon Fourie reviews
General Jan Smuts and His First World War in Africa 1914–1917
By David Brock Katz

Trevor Bedeman reviews
How to Fight a War
by Mike Martin

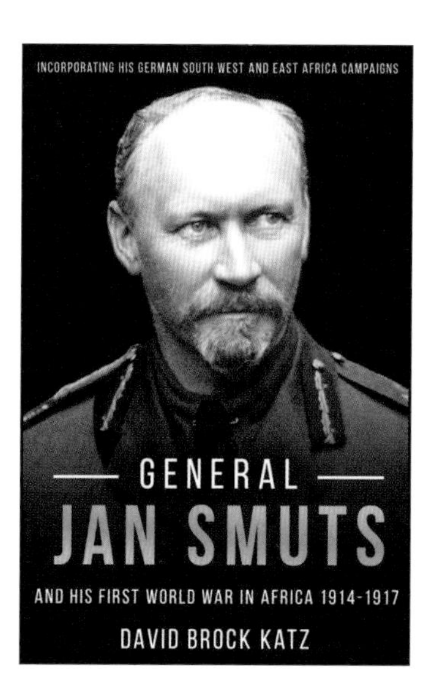

General Jan Smuts and His First World War in Africa 1914–1917

David Brock Katz
Jonathan Ball Publishers, 2022

Although Field Marshal Jan Smuts died in 1950, recent years in South Africa have seen a revived interest in his life and achievements. After South Africans have kept from writing military history for decades, the past 20 years have seen various military publications become surprisingly popular. The publication of books on the two World Wars, the Anglo-Boer and Anglo-Zulu Wars and the more recent 'Border War' in Namibia and Angola has flourished. The publication of works about Smuts, by, among others, Kobus du Pisani and Richard Steyn, seems to suggest a re-evaluation and a different view of his achievements – even among Afrikaners who grew up in an anti-Smuts atmosphere.

David Brock Katz is a prolific and popular writer in this field. A chartered accountant by profession, his interest in warfare was aroused by his being an officer in a Reserve Force regiment, the South African Irish. He was accepted by the Military Academy, a faculty of Stellenbosch University, as an undergraduate student in military history. After some years devoted to part-time academic work, he produced this book as his doctoral dissertation. Thus, unlike most military writers in the field, he is a trained historian. He is a dynamic writer whose intimacy with his subject holds one's attention throughout the work.

Apparently answering a challenge by Bill Nasson, the book begins with a rather substantial load of biographical information before dealing with the subject expressed by its title. This does not detract from Katz's theme, however. The book fills a gap left in most works about Smuts which say little or nothing about his approach to military command. For that reason alone, it is a welcome contribution to military literature.

One should not be discouraged by the book's bulk – of the 382 pages the text is 260 pages long, the rest containing endnotes and a bibliography that are evidence of wide-ranging and profound research. It is enhanced by 24 maps, several tables and a selection of photographs and illustrations.

Katz points out that Smuts's experiences in the South-West and East African campaigns were radically different from those of the Anglo-Boer War in which he earned his spurs as a formation commander. He does not merely describe Smuts's battles against the German Protectorate forces – *Schutztruppen* – in the German territories; he provides interesting and thought-

 © RUSI Journal, Vol. 168, No. 3, 2023 pp. 86–89

provoking analyses of Smuts's military doctrinal approach to warfare.

In his earlier work *South Africans Versus Rommel: The Untold Story of the Desert War in World War II* (Stackpole, 2017), Katz sought to show how South African commanders in the Second World War adapted the Boer commander's ad hoc doctrine to the needs of different campaigns.

Katz points out that Smuts's experiences in the South-West and East African campaigns were radically different from those of the Anglo-Boer War

In the present work Katz describes how the younger, imaginative Boer commanders, such as Louis Botha, J H de la Rey and C R de Wet – who were not trained professionals taught to think as would their professional enemies – avoided both holding ground and frontal attacks. Their operational strategy relied on mobility and manoeuvre. When faced with strong and determined opposing forces they would, for example, withdraw rapidly – all being mounted – hoping to entice the enemy to pursue them. They sought to lead pursuing forces on to open ground, not of the enemy's choosing, where, from cover, they could subject them to rapid and usually accurate fire. Alternatively, while leaving a holding force to engage pursuers, they would use two groups of Boer commandos to envelope the enemy. Relying on directive command and permitting their soldiers to use their initiative, the Boer commanders achieved surprising successes in battle.

Katz explains how in 1913, Smuts as General Louis Botha's minister of defence established the Union Defence Force as a bi-doctrinal force. Inevitably, this followed the recruitment of officers from the former forces of the British colonies of the Cape and Natal and the erstwhile republics of the Transvaal and the Orange Free State. The former manned the artillery and infantry units of the Active Citizen Force (formerly colonial Volunteers), and the latter were mainly the commandos and mounted infantry used in the German South-West and East African campaigns. The former colonial Volunteers were, of course, more accustomed to firm discipline, obedience to orders and a rigid structure. In German South-West and East Africa, several younger Boer officers were colonels and brigadier-generals – for example, C J Brits, M W Myburgh and J L van Deventer – who in 1917 replaced Smuts as commander-in-chief of the British force in East Africa.

The application of the Boer approach to warfare was relatively easy in South-West Africa where, although he commanded Southern Force, Smuts played a significant backroom role. Towards the end of the northward pursuit of the *Schutztruppen*, Botha pressed them towards Tsumeb while they withdrew as though they intended to cross southern Angola to reach the German forces in East Africa. Using the infant SA Aviation Corps to reconnoitre, however, Botha was able to envelope them with Brits and Myburgh's mounted brigades. In this way he made Colonel Viktor Franke's surrender at Otavifontein on 9 July 1915 inevitable.

In the East African campaign, applying the Boer approach was more difficult. Soon after Smuts arrived there, he achieved a resounding victory over the German forces. His success at Kilimanjaro reflected on the British commanders' disasters at Tanga and Salaita Hill. Smuts's new subordinate commanders there were mainly British Regulars, and shared the views expressed by British Staff Officer, Colonel Richard Meinertzhagen, who wrote that he did not understand manoeuvre and never would.

The Regulars held strong objections to Smuts's doctrine of mobility, preferring direct attacks to which they felt bound by the Field Service Regulations. Some saw him as an amateur civilian and some still saw him as one of the 'enemy'. The victory at Kilimanjaro did not add to his popularity among all British Regular officers. Nevertheless, although Smuts failed to completely defeat Colonel Paul von Lettow-Vorbeck, the German commander in German East Africa, he was able to clear the Germans from a large swathe of the territory, four fifths, in a relatively brief time. Until and after Botha sent Smuts to attend the Imperial War Conference in 1917, the German commander was able to successfully drag out operations.

The German commanders in both territories were themselves puzzled by the South Africans' apparent absence of desire to engage in pitched battles and preference for manoeuvre.

Katz continues his book with a brief but interesting description of Smuts's subsequent role as a member of the small committee, called the War Cabinet, especially his role in the establishment of the RAF as an important means of dealing with the German bombing of Britain.

A feature of the book that should be mentioned is Katz's response to a range of writers who, in his view, unjustifiably criticised Smuts's approach to command. Katz delves into an exceptionally substantial number of sources, secondary and primary, so that his rebuttal is impressive and credible.

The book certainly contributes to the education of all readers, especially prospective military commanders

Unfortunately, the book contains several errors in word usage which detract from its professional presentation. Some – such as the use of the Soviet term 'operational art' rather than the Western term 'operational strategy' – reduce the accuracy and clarity of the text.

The book is interesting for its analyses of the differing approaches to warfare of commanders and their reasons for differing. It certainly contributes to the education of all readers, especially prospective military commanders. ■

Deon Fourie is formerly Professor of Strategic Studies at the University of South Africa.

DOI: 10.1080/03071847.2023.2221143

How to Fight a War

Mike Martin

Hurst, 2023

Is it flippant to write a form of handbook on how to fight a war in 2023, and can this be responsibly reviewed in the *RUSI Journal*? I have argued in a previous review that, since the full-scale invasion of Ukraine in 2022, there will need to be new forms of military history to review, especially ones that are not entertainment-driven and which take account of new realities. This handbook sets out many of the challenges of a new era, including war itself along global fault lines. It does this in a clear and approachable way.

Why am I so pleased to have it, and to recommend it to others? The work is probably too general to appeal to experts such as generals and admirals. However, students especially new to the field could well keep it forever, treasuring the various marks that they have made in the margins along the way. This is despite its lack of references which slightly detracts from what is otherwise a candidate for a good basic textbook for defence studies. Even those who work in government are likely to gain from reading this.

Mike Martin argues that war is a psychological act, which someone must make, and someone receive and process. While it is correct, then, to imply that it is thus importantly an emotional act, it seems a step too far to say 'humans are not rational beings, rather emotional beings' (p. 6). This reviewer suggests they are a mixture of both, which varies with the individual and the circumstance. While an important point to dispute at the start of the book, it does not, in practice, reduce its utility.

Making war is a huge subject to fit in to a book of only some 230 pages, but this volume seems to manage to do it succinctly

He is firm in his view that it is the intangibles that need to have priority in warfare when it is taken as a whole. He defines these for Part 1 of the book as strategy/intelligence, logistics, morale and training. Then, for Part 2, he covers the domains which now include space and cyber (computer security), while Part 3 examines the art of using lethal violence.

Making war is a huge subject to fit in to a book of only some 230 pages, but this volume seems to manage to do it succinctly. It is good at indicating how things essential to war fighting have been throughout history, stating that much remains the same, and then pointing out how some familiar things have now become very rare – except in conflicts between certain outmoded states. For example, technology seems to be reducing crewed air-to-air combat, and direct combat between crewed surface ships. But as Martin identifies, the functions of controlling such spaces are still there. While there are question marks over the huge cost of their equipment, the most advanced states have not given up spending vast amounts of money on such crewed assets – in fact, it is quite the reverse. So, he encapsulates a very modern air of uncertainty and change in war planning and fighting.

The author is firm in his view that it is the intangibles that need to have priority in warfare when it is taken as a whole

Another way in which this book is comfortable in its skin, so to speak, is that it is content to define clearly how things are and have been, identify the key questions of the present and the future, but then leave many hanging in the air. I do not think that is the fault of the book – this is a handbook after all, and I suppose that it is designed to help at least some in his audience get a good grounding for the times when they will be forced to come up with the answers.

This handbook illustrates many of these points with practical and carefully chosen examples. For instance, the text shows that the B-52 is such a stable piece of technology that it has lasted for 70 years so far. It can deliver 30 tons of ordnance up to 8,000 miles and has been used in every US war since the 1950s (p. 130).

In contrast, the discussion of uncrewed aerial vehicles shows both the speed of their military development and thus the challenge they make to military powers of all sizes that are unable to keep up. The development and military implications of swarms of drones are discussed here in plain language. As he engagingly points out, the most basic drones can be ordered from Amazon, and used either unadapted for reconnaissance, or easily modified. The supporting developments in computing have been through AI (machine learning and adaptive programming); perhaps this aspect of war could disengage progressively from its human character and become an increasingly industrial and informational conflict.

On cyber (computer security), it is reassuring to hear that one of the forms of alternative and deniable war – 'strategic information operations' – pioneered by Russia, seems to be fading as the West becomes more streetwise. Mark Galeotti recently asked 'is war de-weaponising'? (*The Weaponisation of Everything: A Field Guide to the New Way of War*, 2022, p. 25). The answer from this volume seems to be not as such; rather, the world has become more unstable because of the complexity of quasi-conflict.

On nuclear, chemical and biological weapons, Martin says, 'we are on the cusp of a more unstable world' (p. 164). While the delicate balance of nuclear terror has held based on mutual assured destruction, it is under increasing threat due to the decline in nuclear treaties, the growth of faster delivery missiles and, inevitably, from China's decisions to vastly upgrade its nuclear arsenals. He advises that biological weapons have proved to be difficult to use successfully. Chemical weapons, however, look to have specific military uses: for example, their limited but effective use in urban warfare, which has already also demonstrated the potential for widespread civilian fallout.

The text examines the need for the art of lethal violence. This is the central point of war. It applies to defence in depth, and is especially relevant for offensive infantry engaged in close-quarter combat. While technology is important, it must be underpinned by adequate strategy, morale and logistics.

This handbook illustrates many of these points with practical and carefully chosen examples

Perhaps the most dangerous thing the West did since the end of the Cold War was to not take sufficiently seriously war-making facilities and expenditures, and therefore keep up with the accelerating implications of technical development and increasing forms of instability. This book is to be welcomed and greatly recommended at many levels. ■

Trevor Bedeman is a Partner of London Risk, providing management consultancy for risk and data management. He also founded the Insurance Fraud Bureau and is currently contributing to the development of global reciprocity standards in the sharing of information on economic crime. He is a member of the National Liberal Club Defence and Security Circle.

DOI: 10.1080/03071847.2023.2230029

RUSI Journal Article and Letter Submission Guidelines

The Editor welcomes the submission of unpublished manuscripts on all topics related to UK and international defence and security issues, as well as military history. Authors are requested to consider the following guidelines:

1. Articles should be the author's original work; simultaneous submission to other publications must be indicated.

2. Articles should be relevant to the *Journal*'s defence and security policy focus; clear, analytical pieces are preferred. The *RUSI Journal* is an English-language publication, and jargon and non-English vocabulary should be kept to a minimum.

3. Submissions should be between 3,500 and 6,000 words, and should be fully referenced with complete footnotes. Responsibility for factual accuracy lies with the author.

4. Tables or artwork should be supplied separately as high-resolution files (preferably vector format), and not embedded in the text. Authors must ensure they have permission to use any supplied imagery.

5. Authors should adhere to RUSI house style as far as possible, particularly the formatting of references. The style guide is available at **rusi.org/explore-our-research/publications/rusi-journal/contributor-guidelines**.

6. Please include a short biography with your article and submit your document as a Microsoft Word file. Submissions (including tables and artwork) should be made through the ScholarOne platform which allows authors to track the progress of their manuscript throughout the production process. Details on registering for a ScholarOne account can be found at **rusi.org/explore-our-research/publications/rusi-journal/contributor-guidelines**.

7. All submissions to the *RUSI Journal* are rigorously peer reviewed. The final decision on selection follows assessment by the editorial board. We aim to notify authors of the board's decision within twelve weeks of submission.

8. If selected for publication, articles will be edited to meet the RUSI house style and the Institute reserves the right to make alterations for space and clarity. We regret that the *RUSI Journal* cannot offer payment to authors.

Letters

The Editor welcomes correspondence from readers on articles or reviews, and other matters arising from discussions in the *RUSI Journal*.

Letters should be no more than 700 words. Publication in the *Journal* is at the discretion of the Editor; anonymous letters will not be considered.

Please mark all letters for the attention of the Editor and send via email to **emmad@rusi.org** or to Dr Emma De Angelis, RUSI, Whitehall, London, SW1A 2ET, United Kingdom.

Book Reviews

For information regarding book reviews, please see the panel below. Alternatively, visit **rusi.org/explore-our-research/publications/rusi-journal/contributor-guidelines**.

All specific enquiries regarding book reviews should be sent to the Book Reviews Editor, Edward Mortimer, at **edwardm@rusi.org**. If you would like to submit a book to be considered for review, please address it to: The Book Reviews Editor, Royal United Services Institute, Whitehall, London, SW1A 2ET, United Kingdom.

For more information on submitting to the *RUSI Journal*, please visit: rusi.org/explore-our-research/publications/rusi-journal/contributor-guidelines

Book Review Guidelines

The Book Reviews Editor welcomes the submission of unpublished reviews of important or useful new books on all aspects of defence, security and military history.

Authors are requested to follow the following guidelines.

Content

Reviews should primarily consider the value of the book to practitioners and scholars in the particular subject area. Reviews should not merely summarise the contents of a book, but rather assess its contribution to the subject and literature as a whole. In the case of edited volumes, we ask that reviewers do not analyse each chapter in turn, but rather synthesise the book's debates, perspectives and findings.

Criticism is welcome, but must be fair and supported in detail within the review.

If for whatever reason a contributor is uncomfortable with reviewing a book they have been assigned or offered to do, they should inform the Book Reviews Editor as soon as possible. Likewise, in the interest of impartiality, reviewers should declare any connection or interest to the book they are considering.

Length and Style

RUSI Journal book reviews are generally 700–1,000 words. The precise limit can be agreed on a case-by-case basis with the Book Reviews Editor.

Authors are asked to adhere to the RUSI house style. The style guide is available at **rusi.org/explore-our-research/publications/rusi-journal/contributor-guidelines**.

Submissions and Editing

Please include a short biography at the end of your review. Submissions should be made through the ScholarOne platform which allows reviewers to track the progress of their review throughout the production process. Details on registering for a ScholarOne account can be found at **rusi.org/explore-our-research/publications/rusi-journal/contributor-guidelines**.

The final decision on selection rests with the Book Reviews Editor. Authors can expect to be notified of the Editor's decision within two weeks of submission. If selected for publication, reviews will be edited to meet the RUSI house style and the Institute reserves the right to make alterations for space and clarity. Authors will receive an edited version of their review and also one PDF proof before the *Journal* goes to press. In each case, the author will have 72 hours to send any amends to the Editor.

Payment

Reviewers are not paid. However, they may keep the copy of the book they have been sent and they will receive a courtesy copy of the *Journal* issue in which they are published.

Enquiries

If you would like to suggest yourself as a reviewer for a newly published book, please contact the Book Reviews Editor, Edward Mortimer, at **edwardm@rusi.org**. Please submit all general enquiries to this address also.

If you would like to submit a book to be considered for review, please address it to: The Book Reviews Editor, Royal United Services Institute, Whitehall, London SWIA 2ET.